Sounding out the City

MATERIALIZING CULTURE
. . . .

Series Editors: Paul Gilroy, Michael Herzfeld and Danny Miller

Sounding out the City

Personal Stereos and the Management of Everyday Life

Michael Bull

Oxford • New York

First published in 2000 by
Berg
Editorial offices:
150 Cowley Road, Oxford, OX4 1JJ, UK
838 Broadway, Third Floor, New York, NY 10003-4812, USA

Berg is the imprint of Oxford International Publishers Ltd.

Library of Congress Cataloging-in-Publication Data

A catalogue record for this book is available from the Library of
Congress.

British Library Cataloguing-in-Publication Data

A catalogue record for this book is available from the British Library.

ISBN 1 85973 337 9 (Cloth)
      1 85973 342 5 (Paper)

Typeset by JS Typesetting, Wellingborough, Northants.
Printed in the United Kingdom by Biddles Ltd, Guildford and
King's Lynn.

Contents

Preface

This book analyses the meaning of personal-stereo use in the everyday life of users. However, the attentive reader will discover that in the text users habitually refer to their machines as 'Walkmans', whilst I describe them as 'personal stereos'. There is a relatively simple explanation for this. For whilst I or perhaps you tend to describe a personal stereo as a 'walkman' in everyday discourse, the name is in fact a trademark of the Sony Corporation. This means essentially that they own the name.

Sony were the first company to market personal stereos in 1979. Initially they were not sure what to call these machines but hit on the word 'walkman', which proved a great success. The very success of Sony in establishing the term 'Walkman' to describe personal stereos has produced the need to defend it. A trademark means that other companies cannot market their personal stereo's using the name 'Walkman'. This ownership extends to the commercial use of the term. So whilst this book is not selling personal stereos, it is, nevertheless, a kind of commercial product. With this point in mind, the Sony Corporation were not willing for the author to use the term in either the title of the book or in its content, except verbatim to report what personal-stereo users actually say. Rather than displaying any antipathy towards learned books, Sony appears to be concerned that, by giving permission to use the trademark in this instance, they might thereby compromise their ability to defend that trademark against other companies' use of it in the future. Both terms are interesting in the context of this book: 'Walkman' for its connotation of movement, and 'personal stereo' for its description of the intimate and private nature of use.

Personal Stereos and the Management of Everyday Life: An Introduction

Whenever intellectual formulations are treated simply by relegating them to the past and permitting the simple passage of time to substitute for development the suspicion is justified that such formulations have not really been mastered, but rather that they are being suppressed

T. Adorno, *The Positivist Dispute in German Sociology*

'The community stagnates without the impulse of the individual, the impulse dies away without the sympathy of the community.'

William James quoted in J. Habermas, *Justification and Application*

For twenty five centuries Western knowledge has tried to look upon the world. It has failed to understand that the world is not for beholding. It is for hearing...Now we must learn to judge a society by its noise.

J. Attali, *Noise: The Political Economy of Music*

What? What are you talking about? The Sony Walkman has done more to change human perception than any virtual reality gadget. I can't remember any technological experience since that was quite so wonderful as being able to take music and move it through landscapes and architecture.

William Gibson: *Time Out*

This book is about the first truly mobile consumer technology, the personal stereo. In it I analyse the significance and meaning of personal-stereo use in the everyday life of users. In doing so I ask three main questions: what is the nature and influence of the auditory in everyday life? what role does technology play in the construction of auditory experience? and what role do personal stereos play in the management of the everyday life of users?

Personal-stereo users, in their daily lives, move through a variety of urban spaces, which I argue have a cognitive, aesthetic and moral significance that are all relational in so much as they inform us of the ways in which users relate to their surroundings, others and themselves.[1] However, mainstream accounts of urban behaviour either fail to address how technology, in this instance the personal stereo, impacts upon these three concerns or ignore the specific relational nature of auditory experience in the daily lives of people. Let me go further than this; there is no contemporary account of the auditory nature of everyday experience in urban and cultural studies. By focusing upon the auditory and the technologized nature of everyday experience of personal-stereo users, I explain their attempts at creating manageable sites of habitation and I chart the multifaceted ways in which their experience is transformed and constructed through habitual use. Through a close analysis of the ethnographic material[2] I demonstrate the ways in which personal stereos become a critical tool for users in their management of space and time, in their construction of boundaries around the self, and as the site of fantasy and memory. In doing so I propose to formulate a new moral geography of the city that places the management of contingency and the production of forms of interpersonal asymmetry at the centre of its account.

Sound, the audible, is thus put back onto the cognitive map of urban experience; sound as opposed to vision becomes the site for the critical investigation of urban life, challenging the sufficiency of visually orientated explanations of urban behaviour. In doing so, I highlight the invisibility of sound in the academic literature on the city and everyday life. If the world is for hearing, as Attali suggests, then there exists an unexplored gulf between the world according to sound and the world according to sight. Going down the auditory path requires taking a fresh look at what has been written of the senses, technology and everyday experience. Sound has its own distinctive relational qualities; as Berkeley observed, 'sounds are as near to us as our thoughts' (quoted in Rée, 1999 p.36). Sound is essentially non spatial in character, or rather sound engulfs the spatial, thus making the relation between subject and object problematic. Sound inhabits the subject just as the subject might be said to inhabit sound, whereas vision, in contrast to sound, represents distance, the singular, the objectifying (Jay 1993).

Yet, despite these distinctions, visually based paradigms are used to explain the nature of all urban experience. In these explanations, subjects are perceived to be either retreating from the urban (Simmel 1997), aestheticizing it (Bauman 1991) or are indifferent to it (Sennett 1990). Whilst these positions have considerable explanatory power, the following study highlights the way in which this visual primacy fails sufficiently to explain the relational nature of auditory experience. As these epistemologies of everyday life are amended, so a range of neglected or misunderstood texts will be drawn upon in order to develop an adequate address to the nature of the auditory urban. In doing so I draw upon Lefebvre's understanding of social space together with the early work of the Frankfurt School, whose work on technology and the historical construction of the senses has been largely neglected by writers in the field. This new and rejuvenated critical theory of auditory urban experience is coupled to an ethnography based on a phenomenological understanding of the construction of everyday life. With these theoretical tools I construct a critical phenomenology of auditory urban experience through an analysis of personal-stereo use.

The Personal Stereo: Icon of Mobile Auditory Experience

Personal stereos have, as Gibson noted, revolutionized the everyday experience of millions of people daily as they move through the city. They are first and foremost a very direct and powerful form of technological artifact which re-prioritizes the auditory nature of experience with an unusual directness and immediacy. Mobility is inscribed into the very design of personal stereos, enabling users to travel through any space accompanied by their own 'individualized' soundworld. Since they were introduced by the Sony Corporation in 1979 they have sold consistently in their millions. This success has not been dependent upon massive advertising campaigns and neither are they a fad of the period, like the Rubrik's Cube, for example. The sale of personal stereos continues to grow as they are being used by an increasingly wide user group, beyond teenagers and commuters who use them regularly as part of their daily routine. Personal stereos have become a truly international tool used in New York, Tokyo, Berlin, Paris or any metropolitan environment. Each morning millions of urban inhabitants place a pair of headphones over their heads, or place earpieces directly into their ears, and turn the music on as they leave home. They walk down streets, sit on tubes or buses and keep listening till they reach their destination. They might continue listening on arrival, whether it be furtively at the back of a classroom, one hand over the listening ear, or in their place of work. Many users never go out in public without their personal stereo. On their way home at the end of the day the pattern repeats itself. Yet contemporary urban and cultural theory has not, and I propose cannot, provide an adequate set of explanations to account for personal-stereo use. Personal stereos have indeed remained largely invisible in urban and cultural studies, unlike the massive amount of work generated by the use of other domestic consumer communication technologies such as the television or computer. Moreover, existing accounts fail to adequately explain either the role or use of personal stereos in the everyday experience of users.[3] This inadequacy is indicative of many studies of everyday life found in urban or cultural studies that demonstrate a range of structural weaknesses of explanation which I aim to overcome in the present study of personal-stereo use.[4] These 'structural' problems of explanation are:

1. An unreflective use of visually based epistemologies by which all behaviour is explained.
2. An obsession with explaining the nature of everyday life with a theoretical set of dualisms which themselves derive from these visually based epistemologies. Experience is thus divided into the active or passive, the public or the private, the subject or the object and so on.
3. An increasing tendency to read the meaning of behaviour teleologically from a pre-ordained theoretical base rather than investigating the empirical behaviour itself. Thus everyday behaviour is often derived from postmodern notions of subjectivity in which we are all described as decentred, despatialized beings (Chambers 1994; Hosokawa 1984). Alternatively, traditional theoretical or literary concepts are operationalized to explain contemporary behaviour. In these scenarios we all become latter-day flâneurs (Bauman 1991; Jenks 1995; Tester 1994). Failing this, the meaning of everyday behaviour is read off semiotically from advertising images in which we all become like the image in the advert (du Gay and Hall 1997). In all of these accounts there is a failure to come adequately to grips with the detailed and rich ethnography of everyday life from which potentially new meanings, concepts and frameworks might arise.
4. Alternatively, much empirical work fears to move beyond the merely descriptive and so tends to move within narrow theoretical

frameworks. The study of the living room for example might be seen to bear no relation to the habitation of the street, and so on (Lull 1990). Thus the very notions that might be in need of interrogation, notions of experience, leisure, the public and private often become assumed in otherwise interesting descriptive accounts of experience. These may appear sweeping and provocative claims but they will be substantiated and justified throughout the book.

Studying Personal-Stereo Use

In 1993 when I began investigating personal-stereo use no empirical research had been carried out in any discipline on this subject. Personal stereos had largely passed the academy by. du Gay and Hall (1997) published their story of the Sony Walkman as the centrepiece of a new Open University course on cultural processes. The text was intended to demonstrate 'good practice' in cultural studies, yet paradoxically it lacked any empirical investigation of 'actual' personal-stereo user practices. Whilst a chapter of their book was devoted to personal stereo 'practices', these consisted of repeating the impressionistic, non-empirical, accounts of earlier discussions of personal stereos (Chambers 1994; Hosokawa 1984). The only empirical material referred to was commercially sponsored Mintel research material used by Sony's advertising agency at the time. The need for empirical research, whilst stated as necessary in the text, took a secondary role due to their emphasis on reading the meaning of personal-stereo use through existing advertising images. This despite the relatively minimal advertising exposure of personal stereo's. During the summer of 1993 I spent a week meeting Sony executives in Tokyo where I discovered that the advertising of personal stereos had never been given a high priority by the corporation as after their initial introduction and advertising drive they sold very easily. This was born out in subsequent interviews with Sony's advertising agency, Bartle, Bogle and Hegerty, where I spent two days interviewing the production team. They produced the only two television advertisements of Sony Walkmans to be shown in Britain in the early 1980s. Looking at Sony's advertising plans of the previous years Walkman expenditure was found to be the smallest of all their products. The advertising agency stated the need to keep the brand name in focus as the primary motive for advertising the Sony Walkman. Given the paucity of personal stereo images, a methodology that reads actual use from advertising images appears to be, at best, unhelpful.

Equally, when interviewing designers of Sony Walkmans in Tokyo, in a room that contained every Sony Walkman model produced by Sony worldwide, the Japanese designers were still working on the assumption that personal-stereo users preferred hidden headsets. They were surprised to hear (this was in 1993) that many users in Britain preferred large wrap around headsets, as this contradicted both the notions of listening anonymity and miniaturization that were the assumed categories of the design team. This example tends to support the proposition that their is no inherent functional fit between design and use. Implicit in work that reads off use from advertising imagery is the suggestion of just such a functional fit. In this work I move beyond the workings of advertising producers in developing an understanding of personal-stereo use. I equally move beyond any reductive structural position where any meanings attached to use are read off from advertising images. Whilst images do, of course, tell us much, the position taken in this research is that everyday life is richer, more complex and more contradictory than the understandings of those working in the culture industry who produce this imagery. Equally theoretically sophisticated forms of interpretation of 'imagery' do not necessarily get us closer to the social practices engaged in by subjects in mundane everyday contexts. Hence it is not surprising that work on personal stereos tends to fall back on stereotypical categories of everyday behaviour in which the categories used tend to be self-fulfilling.

In disclosing the world of the auditory urban through personal-stereo use, I draw upon Appadurai's (1986) observation that material artifacts can open themselves up to many forms of investigation in pursuit of an understanding of their social meaning and identity. Traces of their possible meaning are embodied in the very practices that bring them to life. The object is not merely an artifact but also a set of practices with which an artifact is associated. These practices give meaning to the object just as the object discloses something of the user in them. Artifacts also have biographies that extend beyond themselves and which are decipherable by focusing upon the material artifact as a microcosm of the social. Personal stereos, as such, can be understood within the matrix of the social practices carried out through them. The very mobility of its use permits an analysis of the 'seamless web' of daily life. I use personal stereos as a prism through which both its own meanings and the meaning of the acts undertaken through it are to be understood. In doing so the cultural assumptions concerning the nature of the social and the public can be understood through an investigation of the everyday use of personal stereos. The daily strategies of users as they manage their urban experience casts light on the social construction and meaning of that experience. This prismatic approach to knowledge is also located in the early works of Benjamin, Adorno and Kracauer. I use some of their insights in the following pages in order to construct a new critical theory of urban everyday life.

Introducing a Critical Theory of Auditory Urban Experience

If I am correct in my assessment of the inadequacy of visually based accounts of urban experience, can a Critical Theory do any better? Let me be clear about this, I am not proposing to take the work of Adorno, Benjamin and others and merely apply it to contemporary urban experience. Rather I situate their work within an historical constellation that takes account of its periodicity and its lineage. Despite the changes in the nature of experience and technology that has taken place since the 1930s and 1940s, personal-stereo use can be understood as taking its place in the lineage of communication technologies (Freeberg 1993). I thus use Critical Theory within a strategy of 'adjustment through modification' (Hohendahl 1995, p. 244).

Despite the interest shown by some commentators in the relevance of Critical Theory to the understanding of experience, technology and culture, there has been no empirical engagement with Critical Theory to date (Calhoun 1995; Kellner 1995). The present study approaches the subject by engaging with and reworking early themes developed in the work of Benjamin and Adorno and filtering them through an empirical analysis of personal-stereo use. I also broaden out their theoretical work on the senses and experience by drawing upon a wide range of theorists including the contemporary critical theorist Axel Honneth, Henri Lefebvre, Gaston Bachelard and Richard Sennett. In doing so I demonstrate a level of continuity of interest within Critical Theory that 'locates the motivating insight for emancipatory struggle within the domain of ordinary experience' (Anderson in Honneth 1995b, p. xi) and I also locate the theory as a theory of urban experience. In doing so I contest the taken-for-granted assumption of most work on Critical Theory that argues that they give no role to 'agency' in their account of urban experience.

Critical Theorists as early as the 1930s analysed the historical nature of the senses in relation to the use of new forms of communication technologies thus providing a framework for an understanding of these processes that has largely been ignored by contemporary writers.

Contemporary accounts of technologized urban experience often fail to discuss adequately those concerns addressed as early as 1929 by Kracauer in his discussion of early radio use:

> Who could resist the invitation of those dainty headphones? They gleam in living rooms and entwine themselves around heads all by themselves; and instead of fostering cultivated conversation (which certainly can be a bore), one becomes a playground for Eiffel noises that, regardless of their potentially active boredom, do not even grant ones modest right to personal boredom. Silent and lifeless, people sit side by side as if their souls were wandering about far away. But these souls are not wandering according to their own preferences; they are badgered by the news hounds, and soon no one can tell who is the hunter and who is the hunted. (Kracauer 1995, p. 333)

Kracauer provides me with both a tentative theoretical framework and an historical contextualization for the present study of personal stereos. The transformation of experience through the privatized act of listening places personal stereos within an historical trajectory of technologized experience that incorporates the daily use of other communication technologies such as radio, television and film. Kracauer points to the ambiguous and seductive nature of these new domestic communication technologies: 'who could resist the invitation of those dainty head-phones?' But what is it about those headphones that is so attractive? Is it that they wrap themselves snuggly around the head of the user, hinting at some kind of an auditory intimacy? Yet Kracauer is equally concerned with what the technology appears to achieve. His radio users transcend geographical space, listening takes them away from the mundanity of their domestic space. They no longer commune with those in physical proximity to them but with the voices transmitted through the ether which is seen as a better bet than any discussion with the person adjacent to them. The technology of the radio and the headphones enables users to prioritize their experience socially. Kracauer in this description addresses the nature of cognitive, aesthetic and moral spacings of urban life, which I am concerned with in this study, but he does so through the technologization of these realms.

It is no surprise that Kracauer was closely associated with the first generation of Frankfurt theorists who were at that time engaged in the analysis of the camera, film and recorded music in terms of their relational qualities. Kracauer's analysis draws us in to a dialectical understanding of experience. His subjects appear to be retreating into mediated forms of public inwardness which transform both the 'site' and 'horizon' of their experience. It is precisely this transformation which will be investigated in the following analysis of personal-stereo use. Just as Kracauer inquires rhetorically of the relationship between subject and object, the active and the passive, in his depiction of the ambivalent relationship between hunter and hunted, so I will develop these concerns through analysing the daily rituals of personal-stereo users.

In the following chapters I demonstrate how the use of personal stereos changes the nature of the user's cognition and facilitates the effective management of these states together with a range of strategies (technologies) enabling the successful everyday management of space, place and interpersonal experience. Embedded in personal-stereo use are a variety of strategies that enable the user to successfully prioritize their own experience, personally, interpersonally and geographically. In doing so I claim that contingency, like risk, becomes mediated through the structural possibilities of personal-stereo use. In this sense, urban experience becomes, in a significant manner, technological experience. The use of personal stereos provides users with a vastly expanded range of management strategies as they go about their everyday life. My arguments in the following pages are that if everyday behaviour is understood through the experience of sound, then our understanding of our experience of place, space, time will have to be re-evaluated together with the organization of, and our relationship to, our own thoughts, desires and fantasies. Of equal concern is the effort to understand the nature of the moral geography of an auditized urban environment as users attempt to maintain their corporeal identity in the midst of others.

Technologies of sound thus affect our relationship to the spaces we inhabit.[5] Personal-stereo use is different in one very significant way to Kracauer's radio user. Personal stereos are inherently mobile. Just as radio use transforms the space of the living room so personal-stereo use transforms the urban spacings of the street. The transformed social dynamic of the living room is taken out into the street. They also differ from the radio user as they possess their own individualized, yet equally industrialized, auditory world through their choice of music. Personal stereos are that most intimate mode of auditory technology that permit an investigation into the social dynamics of the technology of sound on spatial urban experience.

Equally, the relationship between subject (experiencing subject) and object (cultural forms) are subject to a complex sets of mediations, through personal-stereo use, in which the subjective moment of experience is problematized. As users become habitually orientated to having their own personalized soundworld accompanying them in ever more areas of their everyday life, then we, like Kracauer can ask: who is the hunted and who the hunter? In analysing personal-stereo use the 'dialectical tension between the principle of domination and resistance to the social system' (Hohendahl 1995, p. 8) becomes one of the theoretical cornerstones of the study.

A Phenomenology of Personal-Stereo Use?

The theoretical concerns expressed above will be intimately tied to an ethnography of personal-stereo use. Whilst anthropologists take the need for ethnography as paramount, those working in the fields of cultural and urban studies do not. Hence my criticisms in the earlier section concerning overgeneralized and teleological accounts of every-day behaviour tied to reductive or romanticized notions of the everyday.

Adorno, contrary to received opinion, also recognized the need for empirical work in order to foreclose the reification of those concepts that were themselves meant to unfold or unmask the meanings of forms of experience within the force field of societal determinations.[6] Empirical methodology, as such, is not in opposition to a Critical Theoretical framework. With this issue in mind, the present study draws Critical Theory together with a more ethnographic approach tied to an empirically orientated phenomenological methodology. In doing so I articulate the nature of a moral urban geography understood through personal-stereo use. I follow users as they struggle to maintain their corporeal integrity of self through the technological organization of space and place.

Phenomenology is a method that permits an adequate understanding of users' habitual daily activities as it is attentive to the way in which social meanings are bedded down in individual forms of experience.

> The funded experience of a life, what a phenomenologist would call the 'sedimented' structure of the individual's experience, is the condition for the subsequent interpretation of all new events and activities. (Natanson 1976, p. xxviii)

Phenomenological method lends itself to an investigation of the structure of technologically mediated forms of everyday experience by permitting the dual study of the structure of experience together with the sedimented meanings underlying the daily experience of subjects. The pressing need for proper phenomenological ethnography in studies of everyday life has been called for in the recent work of Silverstone (1994) and Rojek (1995). Incipient forms of phenomenological analysis have also been recognized in the work of Benjamin, thus linking Critical Theory to phenomenology:

> The main themes of this phenomenology of the city are fragmentation, commodification, interiorisation and the marginalisation of experience. Benjamin is engaged in the representation of the city as a 'landscape of noisy life'. (Gilloch 1996, p. 7)

Tacussel equally points to a phenomenology in which Benjamin provides a 'micro-sociology of everyday life in the city' (Tacussel 1986, p. 48). If phenomenology casts light upon that which is overlooked, it appears to be eminently suitable for an investigation of auditory experience. Personal-stereo use possesses a 'veritable dailiness', which is inscribed into the daily rituals of users and this requires a method-ology that can encompass the way users construct this dailiness, without resorting to either mere subjective description or teleological accounts (users are flâneurs etc). Phenomenological analysis in conjunction with a dialectical understanding of experience will enable the present analysis to transcend static concepts of either perceiving people to be passive or active in their everyday life. I follow Rojek in his criticism of work in the field of leisure where he states that:

> Experience tends to be an assumed category in most treatments of leisure under the gladiatorial paradigm. That is, it is 'read off' from a person's sex, race, age, income level, regional location and so forth. The dialectic between differentiation and de-differentiation suggests that everyday experience is more contradictory and many sided than these analytical practices allow. (Rojek 1995, p. 102)

By using phenomenological methodology in conjunction with a reformulated Critical Theory, a serious dialectic is constructed between structure and experience. This is carried out through the development of a critical phenomenology in which a dialectic between forms of intention and contingency is investigated through the mediated nature of personal-stereo use. This critical phenomenology is dialectic, exper-iential and qualitative. The resulting phenomenology is both structural and non-reductive, encompassing both a typology of use and an overview of the everyday practices of users.

By attending closely to how users describe their activity, it is possible to develop a structural framework that incorporates notions of space, place, time, cognition (looking, listening, thinking, remembering) and the interpersonal within a critical framework encompassing the concepts of control, management, contingency and asymmetry. If personal-stereo users both present themselves via technology and construct the social via technology then a critical phenomenology of this experience permits an evaluation of those strategies that permeate the everyday life of users. In doing so I construct an explanatory bridge between the concerns of Critical Theorists, urbanists such as Sennett and Bauman, and writers, like Silverstone, concerned with the way in which consumer technologies become part of everyday life.

In sounding out the nature of urban experience the study:

1. Proposes a re-evaluation of the significance of the auditory in everyday experience and a re-assessment of the role and relation of the senses within urban experience;
2. Provides an original re-assessment of the placing of technology in everyday experience;
3. Re-integrates the work of the early Critical Theorists (Adorno, Benjamin etc) into a contemporary account of the relation between technology, the urban and everyday experience;
4. Demonstrates how qualitative empirical material (case studies/thick description) can be used to formulate new theoretical frameworks and explanations of urban behaviour. This ethnography will demonstrate the usefulness of using a phenomenological framework within which to formulate the ethnographic material. In this way the study joins notions of agency to structure.

The organization of this book is as follows. Chapters Two through to Eight provide the reader with a detailed phenomenologically inspired ethnography of personal-stereo use. Chapters Nine through to Twelve provide a theoretical evaluation of the ethnographic material contextualizing personal-stereo use within debates concerning the organization and management of everyday life expressed above. Readers might prefer to read chapter Nine before the ethnography as it outlines an urban auditory epistemology of everyday life.

Notes

1. 'Social space ought to be seen as a complex interaction of three inter-woven, yet distinct processes – those of cognitive, aesthetic and moral "spacings" and their respective products.' (Bauman 1991, p. 145)

2. The study was carried out primarily in London over a two-year period, from 1994 to 1996 and consisted of in-depth qualitative interviews with over sixty personal-stereo users. Interviews were conducted both with individual users and in groups. Supplementary material was gained through the use of diaries. Subjects represented a cross-section of users in terms of age, gender, ethnicity and occupation.

3. Despite the growing body of research into how new forms of commun-ication technologies are incorporated into the daily lives of users, there has been very little attention paid to the ways in which personal stereos are used on a routine basis. Invariably, analysis is impressionistic and anecdotal (Chambers 1994). No empirical work on use has been published with the exception of a small piece of work carried out by German psychologists Moebius and Michel-Annen (1994) who locate the meaning of use in the psychological disposition of users thereby reifying both users and use into static categories and ignores the mediating effect of culture and technology on usage. In contrast to this, the recent work of du Gay and Hall (1997) represents the only sustained attempt to analyse the meaning of personal stereos. Whilst they present a very detailed account of the genesis of the Sony Walkman they tend to situate the artifact within the design strategies of Sony and its meaning through an analysis of public representations of use through advertisements. They thus prioritize advertising images from which cultural meanings and forms of usage are read, resulting in a 'stereotypical' description of uses and 'users' which fails to attend to the complexity of use. The work of Hosokawa (1984) and Chambers (1994) situate personal-stereo use within forms of urban social contestation and de-centred experience drawing theoretically upon the work of De Certeau (1988), and Deleuze and Guattari (1987). Users become 'nomadic rebels' or 'flâneurs' experientially remaking their urban experience aesthetically as de-centred subjects. These claims are never tested against any empirical analysis of use and result in a romanticization of both users and the nature of much urban experience.

4. The limitations of existing work on personal stereos and their use is symptomatic of much research undertaken in the field of communication technology, experience and urban culture which often falls into familiar dichotomous theoretical and empirical frameworks. Many contemporary accounts of urban behaviour, for example, either fail to adequately address

the everyday lifeworlds of subjects or, if discussed, restrict the analysis to a positive description of activity that goes no further than the subjective description of that behaviour. I refer to this as the 'valedictory' school of thought that appears to associate 'agency' mimetically with subversion or liberation, in which categories of thought and action that are themselves in need of interpretation are taken as 'given' (Chambers 1994; Fiske 1989). We require a theory of urban experience that is attentive to the historical and culturally situatedness of notions such as 'agency' , 'experience', the 'visual' and the 'auditory'. These categories, I argue, often have ambiguous experiential meaning attached to them and should not be used as coat-hangers upon which to drape either description or abstract theorizing. An intellectual division of labour appears to exist in much urban theory in which the role of commun-ication technologies are rarely discussed, whilst research on the use of communication technologies more often than not remains within the confines of the living room (Lull 1990). The technologizing of experience therefore appears to occur in the home or office only to drift away in public spaces. Those studies that do discuss the street equally fall back on largely visually based frameworks that derive from the a selective reading of the work of Simmel. Researching everyday urban behaviour therefore appears to suffer either from a deficiency of theoretical acumen or from a lack of empirical grounding from which the categories constructed could be critically developed to provide new insights into everyday practices.

5. Whilst personal-stereo users normally listen to music on their machines, it is not my concern to discuss types of music but rather to discuss the role of personal stereos, as a piece of communication technology, in the construction of mundane everyday experience. Music is a most powerful sensory stimulator and the technology of personal stereos cannot be easily disentangled from the technology of sound listened to through them. However the structural placing and role of the personal stereo in everyday experience can be analytically distinguished from that which is listened to. Of greater significance to this study is the fact that something is being listened to in specific urban contexts. As such, this book aims to study the auditory re-prioritization of forms of urban experience. So whilst users describe music as an activating force facilitating a variety of feelings and describe their fantasies to music or perhaps speech I am more concerned with the role of personal stereo's in the con-struction and transformation of experience.

Adorno's empirical work in the 1940s at Princeton was largely concerned with the structure of listening, although he was also concerned with the mediated nature of reception and specifically its spatial and acoustic properties. He recognized both the difficulty of creating an adequate methodology and the necessity of it in relation to 'the difficulty in verbalising what music subjectively awakens in the listener, the utter obscurity of what is blithely called "the lived experience of music"' (Adorno 1998, p. 220). Whilst positing the need for 'qualitative case studies' (Adorno 1998, p. 221), he himself, during his period in America, confesses to being 'unable to devise questionnaires and interview schemes that at least addressed the essential points.' (Adorno 1998, p. 223) He did, however, produce 'a kind of phenomenology of hit songs' for the *Kenyon Review* at this time.

My phenomenology of personal-stereo use, whilst orientating itself to a dialectical understanding of the phenomena in locating use as part of societal mediation, does not locate itself within the explanatory framework that Adorno developed in the 1940s. Whilst I accept Adorno's prognosis that most music works and functions as a commodity for the user, my orientation is tangential to that of Adorno. Adorno's work was concerned primarily with modes of listening in which he connected the manner of reception to musical form which itself was socially and historically situated. In doing this he developed a typology of listening (not listeners) characterized by notions of the fetishization of music used as compulsive background sound or as forms of emotional stimulation. Those writers who have discussed Adorno's sociology of music, primarily Paddison (1993) and Witkin (1998), focus more on the structure of music as a sociological phenomenon, following Adorno, than on the structural and spatial understanding of the phenomena located as a form of the urban everyday. Whilst my work bears out Adorno's claims to some extent I focus more upon the relational mode of urban experience within which auditory experience forms a central place. Hence this work is not about analysing certain pieces of music in relation to the construction of specific thoughts, emotions and such like, but rather to the role of a mediated, privatized and industrialized auditory in the management of users' everyday lives.

6. Indeed Critical Theorists themselves had empirically investigated the rise of new communication technologies providing a useful contextualization to the present study. The oft-repeated claim that Critical Theorists were not interested in empirical research belies much of their early work in the field (Fromm 1984). Adorno's work on radio and television of the 1940s and 1950s (Adorno 1941a, 1941b, 1945) has been largely ignored in the literature on culture and technology, with even those writers sympathetic to Critical Theory claiming a lack of empirical interest in the work of Adorno. Whilst there is some justice in this claim, Adorno was not primarily interested in empirical work, *per se*; it nevertheless underplays both his concern with empiricism as a method and his own empirical work. In his work, carried out largely as part of the Princeton Project, Adorno was keen to develop a frame of analysis within which to discuss the meaning of the everyday use of new technologies. His well-known criticism of empiricism, repeated in detail in his dispute with Karl

Popper (Adorno 1976b), lay in the fact that he had carried out his research under a label he referred to as 'administrative research'. As such, Adorno saw his own early research as functioning to aid the dissemination of 'high culture' rather than in critically interrogating it. Adorno was clear both on the need for empirical work in the field of mass communication and the need for a rigorous dialectical methodology:

> Empirical investigations, even in the domain of cultural phenomena, are not only legitimate but essential. But they should not be hypostatised and treated as a universal key. Above all, they themselves must terminate in theoretical knowledge. Theory is not merely a vehicle that becomes superfluous as soon as the data are available. (Adorno 1998, p. 228)

Adorno was well aware of the need to locate subjective experience empirically within a larger matrix of social constraint. The relationship between subject (experiencing subject) and object (cultural forms) are subject to complex sets of mediations in Critical Theory where the subjective moment in experience is perceived to be necessarily fractured and ambivalent:

> Experience, which, because of its transcendence into individual consciousness, would tempt me to hypothesise it as being absolute. Dialectics is able to legitimise itself by translating this content back to the experience from which it arose. But this is the experience of mediation of all that is individual through the objective societal totality. (Adorno 1976b, pp. 9–10)

The World of Personal-Stereo Users: An Introduction

I wear it all the time, like a pacemaker! A life support machine! It's like I'm a walking resource centre.

Jade: interview number 13

In the following pages I provide an overview of daily personal stereo practices, which will contextualize the following chapters where I discuss discrete areas of personal-stereo use such as the management of space, time, cognition and interpersonal behaviour. Personal-stereo users habitually manage their daily life through the use of an increasing range of communication technologies. Personal stereos might be conceived of as an urban tool used by 'urban' dwellers enabling users to extend their mediated behaviour into many environments previously inaccessible to privatized listening. Personal stereos often migrate with users to other non-urban places such as the beach, the mountain or the sky. They are invariably used on the move: on foot, bicycle, or on buses, trains, tubes and sometimes even in cars. Mostly use is solitary, although teenagers sometimes share their headphones to listen to music. People wait at bus stops, in airport lounges idling the time away, go shopping with them, take them on holiday, wear them on aeroplanes and take them to the beach. Latterday 'flâneurs' stand in Oxford Street holding up placards, for the duration, advertising the latest half price sale whilst listening to their personal stereo. Sports people run to them, take them swimming, skiing, deep-sea diving or gliding. Use is not, however, always a public activity; users may go to sleep with them on, iron to them, walk around the house with it, avoid discussion through it and even make love accompanied to it. Structurally, personal stereos allow users to take their own 'personalized' sounds with them virtually anywhere and this distinguishes it from any other form of music reception. It is invariably a private experience yet paradoxically represents one that is invariably 'floodlit' in its interpersonal resonance. Urban sounds that are democratically intrusive are replaced by alternative urban sounds chosen by the user. This replacement of one soundscape with another changes the users' relation to the urban environment, themselves and others together with their sense of presence and time. This chapter now moves to situate the reader within the phenomenological world of users. In doing so it will construct a narrative through a composite picture of use.[1]

Users wake up to sound. They normally have music on whilst getting ready for the day, whether it be their stereo system or their favourite radio station. Many users will have gone through their rituals of selecting their tapes and recharging their batteries the night before. Personal stereos have their place in the home and have a variety of attendant daily activities attached to their use. The following house is a well stocked house:

> Everybody in the house has a Walkman and we have a shelf. The Walkman, because we don't use tapes in the house, we tape CDs principally for the Walkman you see. So there's a shelf in the house for all of the tapes, the Walkmans and the stock of batteries. (Sue: interview number 61)

Some users will have determined the night before what their tape of the day will be whilst others rather wait to see what mood they are in, or alternatively may rather be swayed by what they hear in the morning on the radio. Others will look frantically through their tapes in order to find the 'right one' to match their mood:

> I spend quite a while thinking what tape to take with me and it really gets me annoyed because if I'm in a rush I think: 'Take anything. You like them all! They're all your tapes!' I can't. It has to be something I really want to listen to. I wouldn't like to take something that would change my mood. I just take something that would fit my mood. (Catriona: interview number 14)

For other users this never poses a problem as they might only use three or four tapes in a year on their personal stereo, invariably using just the one tape for a period of weeks or months. For many users the choice of music is important and is more selective or specific than that which is listened to in the home:

I find that music is a very personal thing and I mean especially on a Walkman. You're taking all the ones you really like and all the personal tracks, putting it on a disc tape and listening to it out of choice on your Walkman. So I think that the music you listen to on a Walkman is more personal than that which you listen to at home. (Sue: Interview number 61)

Invariably, many users have special tapes containing music only listened to on their personal stereo. This music might have some personal association for them functioning as an 'auditory mnemonic' or alternatively might merely put them in the desired mood for the journey or day ahead. The following user is typical when he states:

If I'm in a bad mood then I'll get my Walkman. I've got this heavy rock thing and I'll play that. I try to sustain the mood by forwarding. When I wake up in the morning (listening to the radio) the first song I hear on the radio is the song that will go in my mind the whole day. So I play my Walkman and try to get rid of that song. I'll play my favourite song in the morning, of the tape that I'm listening to, and then I suppose I keep forwarding, rewinding it. (Jade: interview number 13)

Users also aim to minimalize internal cognitive contingency:

I only have, maybe, four tapes that I listen to on a Walkman and two of them are very kind of, specific or particular, are kind of essential tapes. One is more calming and the other more motivating – never fails to do the trick . . . If I'm stressed or not knowing where I'm at or ever. I listen to those two tapes and it always, always guarantees to work . . . It keeps me on track. (Karin: interview number 18)

The metaphor of keeping 'on track' is instructive as it indicates a joining together of mood and duration. By keeping on track the subject reduces the contingency of the relationship between desired mood and time. Maintenance of mood or the need to be in a particular frame of mind features prominently in users' accounts. Some users desire merely to listen, immersing themselves in the tape until they know it completely. They often describe feelings of pleasure when they discover something 'new' in a familiar tape. Many users also desire to take something that is familiar with them whilst outside in order that it might share the journey or day with them. For regular users the idea that they might go outside without music is often described as distressing, as is the failure of the personal stereo to function correctly in use. Other users may decide not to use it on a particular journey but nevertheless prefer to have it with them 'just in case'. The 'just in case' also extends to having spare tapes to cover the possibility of mood changes, thereby minimizing the possibility of not having the 'right' tape to play. Failure to have the correct music invariably makes the personal stereo dysfunctional, leading users to switch their machines off as a preferable alternative to listening to 'incorrect music'. Incorrect is defined in terms of the sounds not matching either the mood of the user, or their surroundings. The user's daily plan might also take into account possible alternative moods or the circumstances of their return journey home later in the day or evening. Users might divide the day into activation times in the morning to calming ones in the evening. If users desire to maintain their mood irrespective of their surroundings or time of day then the same tape tends to be used continually as in the following case:

> It was just the same one and I listened to it over and over again. It was really nice listening to something over and over again.(Amber: interview number 28)

The facility to 'repeat' transforms the ability of the user to maintain their mood by permitting them to remain 'static' within the flow of time and place.

Users habitually turn their personal stereos on the moment they leave their homes or sometimes even before. Regular users almost never leave their homes without it, even if to venture out into the streets for a very short time as these two young users demonstrate:

> I use it more now, even just down the local phone box, you know. I'm lodging at the moment at a house in Lowerburn and even just walking down the phone box – in they go. (Paul: interview number 37)

> I listen to it so ardently, that, the Walkman, whatever I do, whatever I do. I'll be in the kitchen, washing or eating. I'll have it on. I go downstairs to put the heating on. I'll listen to it. Or I go across the road to ask the neighbour for some milk or something. Then I'll still listen to it. Just for that short journey. (Ron: interview number 58)

Personal stereos often become an habitual form of urban accompaniment for city users.

In the Street

Out in the street many users concentrate on getting themselves activated and often describe this in terms of 'hitting' the day positively. Users describe needing something to get them 'going':

In the mornings I'll tend to listen to that sort of stuff (Hard Core) and it really wakes me up. (Kim: interview number 25)

You put a track that's made you feel good in the past. You sort of wake up. It gives you adrenalin. (Sara: interview number 50)

You need a rhythm. Chart music. It's always got a beat. (Frank: interview number 56)

Yeh. I need some sort of aerobics music. (Betty: interview number 34)

The physical environment of the street is invariably described in neutral terms by users, if mentioned at all. Users are much more attentive to their own mood and orientation which is facilitated by sound being pumped through the personal stereo in harmony with their desired mood, orientation or surroundings. Personal stereos are invariably played with sufficient volume to drown out the industrialized sounds of the city. The following commuter explains the necessary strategies for maintaining the pleasure of listening whilst travelling on the tube:

I need to have it loud because of all the noise and all that. It's the loudest on the tube. More often than not it's on so loud I can't hear anything. (Matt: interview number 19)

Personal-stereo use is often in contest with the sounds of the urban environment with users having to be attentive to changing sound levels within their environment in order to maximize their self-orientated experience. A 27-year-old commuter explains this dynamic in the following manner:

Even the loudest of loud. My headphones aren't that good that they cut out all the sound. You've got to be able to hear something. I just have it as loud . . . I try to drown out as much extraneous sound. You find that loud motorcycles and police sirens, but the rest is blocked out. (Stephanie: interview number 42)

Personal-stereo use reorientates and re-spatializes experience which users often describe in solipsistic and aesthetic terms. They describe the personal stereo as providing them with an invisible shell within which the boundaries of both cognitive and physical space become reformulated:

> I think it creates a sense of kind of aura. Sort of like. Even though it's directly in your ears you feel like it's all around your head because you're coming. Because you're really aware it's just you. Only you can hear it. I'm really aware of personal space. My own space anyway . . . I find it quite weird watching things that you normally associate certain sounds with. Like the sounds of walking up and down the stairs or tubes coming in or out. All those things that you hear. like when you've got a Walkman on you don't hear any of those. You've got your own soundtrack. You see them and it looks like they're moving differently because you've got a rhythm in your head. The way that they walk, they flow past you more. (Karin: interview number 18)

In this example the users 'horizon' of experience is described auratically whereby representational space is transformed into 'spectacle'.[2] This aestheticization of experience may well represent a monumentalization of experience in which experiential contingency is negated.[3] This perfection of control is described in the following terms:

> It enables me to sort of bring my own dreamworld. Because I have familiar sounds with my music that I know and sort of cut out people around me. So the music is familiar. There's nothing new happening. I can go into my perfect dreamworld where everything is as I want it. (Magnus: interview number 21)

In contrast to the above example the following user describes her experience in terms of a cognitive control that extends no further than the maintenance of her mood.

> I'm locking myself in a bit more. It locks the rest of the world out. Because it locks the outside world out. You don't feel anxiety. I feel less stress. I relax on the bike. It desensitizes any pain or stress that I might be feeling. It just takes me away. (Robina: interview number 35)

Personal stereos are multifaceted transformative devices for users. Their use may give an added physical presence to a subject's sense of interiority often achieved through the very physicality of the music, whilst at the same time displacing the sounds associated with the movements and activity of the everyday. Users describe these experiences in terms of the strangeness and dreamlike quality of the urban. This disjunction between the sounds in a subject's head and their perception of the outside can sometimes result in greater concentration in which the awareness of their inability to hear commonplace occurrences such as traffic noise or announcements is described as making them more visually attentive. Users may have to decipher clues as to what might be going on around them. This is especially pronounced in the case of cyclists who wear personal stereos in situations where it is necessary to replace their loss of hearing with an acute sense of sight. Yet equally common are users accounts of 'losing' themselves in public and of becoming distracted or disorientated. This is described in terms of moving around in a 'trance-like state' with their perceived reactions to the environment slowed down and their response times to situations subsequently longer:

> Sometimes when I'm listening to my Walkman I just seem to lose all my senses. I forget to look when I cross the street and my reactions become really slow. Yesterday I was trying to cross the road and I just wasn't paying attention and I had my Walkman on. I hate this kind of feeling I have in becoming slow in all my reactions . . . I just daydream all the time. (Catriona: interview number 14)

The movement from one soundscape to another frequently seems to have a jarring effect on the user especially if it is unexpected, as the following cyclist describes:

> I was cycling from Kings Cross down Charing Cross Road and the taxi driver, I could see it happening and, um, he just cut me off. I knew it was going to happen. The handlebars were caught between the bus and the taxi but I didn't come off. But it twisted the handlebars . . . I stayed on, I was fumbling with the Walkman, to get back to reality, to shout at him. I wanted to hear what he said. I was f'ing and blinding . . . I couldn't hear his response with the music on so I was fumbling, trying to find the on/off switch. I pulled on to the side, rearranged myself and put the headphones back and went away again . . . a bit more cautious. (Ben: interview number 41)

This description of being rooted to the spot is not based on fear but represents the difficulty experienced of switching into an appropriate mode of response whilst having a private experiential world still in operation. The movement from private experience to appropriate social action is often achieved with difficulty. Users often describe having to switch off their personal stereos before responding adequately.

Personal-stereo users like to construct familiar soundscapes to accompany them through their urban journeys. They often describe this in terms of never leaving 'home'. The use of a personal stereo represents something that is both individual and intimate helping them to maintain a sense of identity within an often impersonal environment. Thus, the use of 'meaningful tapes' reminds them of the significance of their own biography in spaces devoid of interest and significance. Use can be understood as facilitating a 'memory bank' of 'significant narratives' by providing an aural mnemonic whilst users move through the 'alien' spaces of daily life. The prominence given to the personal narrative taking place conceptually in the users 'own space' represents a reappropriation of the past in the present whilst the present is experienced as 'removed'. Theirs is a private narrative actively reconstructed in public but shrouded in a form of public invisibility that produces in the user a tentative invulnerability.

Urban environments, however, are not always perceived as alien. Users are just as likely to use their personal stereos in 'friendly' or known environments demonstrating that users are not always responding to the outside urban environment but to their own cognitive and emotional predispositions. Personal-stereo use enhances experience providing the mundane with an exiting, sensual or spectacular soundtrack. Alternatively, users may reconstruct their experience through the construction of imaginary scenarios in which they are either spectators or performers. Throughout all these examples, users describe use as enhancing their sense of control, both internally and externally.

Strategies of everyday management are intrinsic to personal-stereo use and whilst some users have a heightened sense of presence, other users attempt to block out thoughts, or any sense of presence in order to 'go with the flow' of the music. In doing so, unwanted or uncontrollable thoughts are often blocked out. In these situations use can act as an emotional stabilizer to the person producing the desired state of mind. This 'correct' frame of mind enables them to successfully confront whatever the day holds for them. Many users, for example, report arriving at work in a much better frame of mind after using their personal stereo.

In these daily strategies of management, time is also repossessed and made 'their own'. Commuters going to and from work extend ownership of their time through the use of their personal stereo and often report that time becomes more 'productive' and 'pleasurable' for them in doing so. The environment, along with work, is perceived as something 'other' remaining out of their control, or alternatively is thought of as merely 'boring', 'meaningless' or 'unpleasant'. Personal-stereo users move through these spaces, either by withdrawing to be at 'home' with themselves or by aesthetically recreating their experience whereby a personalized fiction is created from the environment. They may, of course, merely treat the time of the journey as leisure time. Through such use public spaces invariably become both transformed and personalized.

Personal stereos tend to be non-interactive in the sense that users construct fantasies and maintain feelings of security precisely by not interacting with others or the environment. Users rather construct a range of interpersonal strategies that are inherently asymmetrical. Ways of auditized looking are developed which are inherently non-reciprocal, functioning to bolster the user's sense of power and control in urban space. Users often approach the public one step removed and this affects how they interact and respond to situations that confront them. Those who travel on the tube, for example, often engage in transformed modes of 'looking' in which their 'look' becomes impervious, thus putting them into an imaginary position of social control or definition which I refer to as a form of 'non-reciprocal gazing'. Alternatively, users withdraw into themselves due to fatigue, boredom or through the desire to have music feature as an all-encompassing facet of their journey. Personal-stereo use enables the users to successfully ignore the environment traversed. The following description comes from a young female secretary travelling home on the tube after a day's work:

> If I'm quite tired it just washes over me. It's background. It's something to drown out the noise of the train. If you want, just want to switch off and be in a room of your own you put that on and you close your eyes and shut your ears and it's a way of not being interrupted. (Mags: interview number 31)

Another user describes using her personal stereo to walk home after work:

> It just seems one minute I'm walking; the next minute I'm there. I don't notice when I'm listening to things. I just appear. I just end up there. I'm not thinking about where I'm going because I'm used to it. My feet just take me there. (Catherine: interview number 3)

Personal-stereo use is one way of dealing with the mundane and repetitive conditions of the everyday. It injects a level of satisfaction into the everyday otherwise unobtainable for the individual. It also enables them to overcome the perceived obstacles of milling crowds and the noises of the city. Personal stereos can also be used as a form of conversational preserve, delimiting who the user wishes to converse with. On an everyday level, the use of a personal stereo is a method of not attending to interactional possibilities.

Users inhabit industrialized sound worlds whether in the home, at work, or in the street. Listening to recorded music or the radio is also to receive industrialized sound. Sound becomes an habitual companion to users' lifeworld with personal-stereo users frequently referring to feelings of unease when there is nothing but 'natural' sound, unadorned around them. The 'silence' of normal sounds is often experienced negatively, as something to be filled in:

> I don't like the silence. I hate it at night. I suppose it's night and you're on your own. I just don't like being alone. I just have to have someone with me or if not with me some type of noise. That's why I have the music on for. (Donna: interview number 52)

In a world filled with noise, rather than craving for silence, users demand their own noise to drown out the fear associated with a silence that throws the user back into their own state of being. Users, in this instance, might be described as being absorbed in the comfort of their own 'forgetting' (Heidegger 1978). Equally the personal stereo forms a cocoon into which the user slips so as to drift into a peaceful and untroubled sleep in communion with the auditized sounds of the ether – in Adorno's terminology into a state of privatized 'we-ness'.[4]

This introductory sketch of use suggests that a complex range of issues concerning place, space, time and the everyday meaning and management of daily experience mediated through the technology of sound is involved in the use of personal stereos. In the following chapters, by developing a phenomenology of personal-stereo use the study formulates an adequate address to the everyday technological urban auditory.

Notes

1. By concentrating on analysing the 'structure' of personal-stereo use it should not be implied from this that anything resembling an 'essentialist'

caricature of a typical user will be created. This misses the main objective of a phenomenological analysis which aims to articulate the qualitative nature of everyday life without limiting itself to localized description. The ethnographic material is used in order to go beyond the individual into structures of use which are then related to the wider social and historical characteristics of society.

Not all personal-stereo users are the same. Indeed it is a central concern of this work to dispute the notion of typical users found in previous research. People use personal stereos like many other forms of communication technology for a variety of reasons and in a variety of circumstances. Whilst it is possible to describe some users as more controlling of their environment and mood than others, it will not be the purpose of the subsequent chapters to develop profiles of users under general categories such as the stroller, dreamer, comfort user, as do Moebius and Michel-Annen (1994). Close analysis of interview material demonstrates a more complex set of uses with each user engaging in a multiple set of uses, motivations and responses. Use therefore does not necessarily render itself susceptible to linear and non-contradictory analysis as the same user may at times withdraw from the public through the production of dream states and at other times confront the social spaces of the city in a confrontational or aggressive manner. For this reason the analysis will focus upon topologies of use rather than a typology of users.

An alternative possible criticism of this methodology is that it might be perceived as flattening out the meanings relating to the diversity of usage. For example, there are important elements of personal-stereo use that could be understood within an analysis of subculture, gender or race. Whilst I recognize the significance of much interesting work carried out in the above fields (Duncan 1996) the aim of this book is not one of subcultural analysis. Therefore, the gendered use of technology or differential use of urban space according to ethnicity or gender is not specifically addressed under these headings. For example, whilst more female users than male describe using personal stereos to avoid unwanted interpersonal communication, I investigate this under the rubric of the 'interpersonal' and the 'look', analysing them as strategies of use. In terms of gendered use, personal-stereo use is distinctive in that it can free itself from restricted forms of geographical location. The ethnographic material indicates, for example, that in some domestic situations personal stereo use can be understood in terms of the expression of a sexual politics with male users controlling discourse in the home in accordance with research into other forms of domestic technologies (Morley 1992). However, the most significant aspect of personal-stereo use is its solitary and non domestic nature. Indeed personal stereos are sometimes used as a strategy to transcend the gendered nature of urban space thus potentially empowering women, enabling them to control space and vision more successfully.

Equally, a subcultural use of personal stereos might focus upon specific types of music used in relation to fashion and social activities whereas a phenomenologically orientated interpretation situates interest in the mere fact that music is listened to in certain everyday situations.

2. Lefebvre uses this term by which he means:

> Space as directly lived through its associated images and symbols, and hence the space of 'inhabiters' and 'users' . . . This is the dominated – and hence passively experienced – space which the imagination seeks to change and appropriate. It overlays physical space, making symbolic use of its object . . . Representational space is alive: it speaks. It has an effective kernel or centre: Ego, bed, bedroom, dwelling house; or square, church, graveyard. It embraces the loci of passion, of action and lived situations . . . It may be directional, situational or relational, because it is essentially qualitative, fluid and dynamic. (Lefebvre 1991b, pp. 39–42)

3. Monumentalization is a term used by Walter Benjamin to describe the denial of the contingent and the passage of time. Benjamin originally used it to discuss the relation of the subject to the object in fascist Germany. Through Nazi propaganda subjects would monumentalize the state and the 'timeless' icons of its identity. As Caygill observes:

> The same photographic technology that in the hands of Atget could open itself to contingency was also capable of re-creating aura and fixing the image of a monumental present. Instead of transforming experience by making it contingent and open to future interpretation, technology may well serve to monumentalize it. (Caygill 1998, p. 95)

In the text I use this term to highlight the way in which personal-stereo users tend to monumentalize their experience through the auditory as an everyday experiential strategy. This does not mean that it has similar political import to Benjamin's discussion of it. I understand monumentalization in terms of the subject's own experience, yet constructed through the personalization of music.

4. 'We-ness' is a process described somewhat unsystematically as a state of 'being with' by which Adorno refers to the substitution of direct experience by technologically mediated forms of experience. I understand this term to refer to a qualitative relationship between the subject and that which is experienced.

Part I

Personal-Stereo Use and the Management of Space, Place and Time

Reconfiguring the 'Site' and 'Horizon' of Experience

Inhabited space transcends geometrical space.

G. Bachelard *The Poetics of Space*

. . . Aura is inseparable from ritual. Ritual . . . is a form of technology, a means of organising and controlling the environment.

H. Caygill *Walter Benjamin*

Personal stereo use reorientates and re-spatializes the users' experience with users often describing the experience in solipsistic and aesthetic terms. Personal stereos appear to provide an invisible shell for the user within which the boundaries of both cognitive and physical space become reformulated. I begin this section of the phenomenology with an analysis of the way in which personal-stereo users inhabit space.

> I don't necessarily feel that I'm there. Especially if I'm listening to the radio. I feel I'm there, where the radio is, because of the way, that is, he's talking to me and only me and no one else around me is listening to that. So I feel like, I know I'm really on the train, but I'm not really . . . I like the fact that there's someone still there. (Mandy: Interview number 43)

Personal-stereo users often describe habitation in terms of an imaginary communion with the source of communication. Mandy is twenty-one. She spends four hours each day travelling across London and uses her personal stereo throughout this time. She likes to listen to both the radio and to taped music on her machine. She listens to music habitually, waking up to it and going to sleep to it. Her description of

31

listening sheds some light upon the connections between technology, experience and place. Using a personal stereo appears to constitute a form of company for her whilst she is alone, through its creation of a zone of intimacy and immediacy. This sense of intimacy and immediateness, following Adorno, appears to be built into the very structure of the auditory medium itself. The headphones of her machine fit snuggly into the ears to provide sound which fills the space of cognition. The 'space' in which reception occurs is decisive, for just as the situation of the television in the home changes the structuring of experience there, so the use of a personal stereo changes the structuring of experience wherever it is used. Mandy describes herself as being where the 'music' or the 'DJ' is. She constructs an imaginary journey within a real journey each day. The space of reception becomes a form of 'mobile home' as she moves through the places of the city. The structuring of space through personal-stereo use is connected to other forms of communication strategies enacted through a range of communication technologies. Users live in a world of technologically mediated sounds and images. The imperative towards experiential states of 'we-ness' is usefully thought of as learnt and embedded in the consumption of television, radio and music reception in the home and elsewhere. The desire for mediated forms of technologized experience becomes part of the sedimented meaning structure of users' everyday experience. This is demonstrated in the following remark by Mandy:

> I can't go to sleep at night without my radio on. I'm one of those people. It's really strange. I find it very difficult. I don't like silence. I'm not that sort of person. I like hearing things around me. It's like hearing that there's a world going on sort of thing. I'm not a very alone person. I will always have something on. I don't mind being by myself as long as I have something on. (Mandy: interview number 43)

Mandy goes on to describe her feeling of centredness, of being secure with her personal stereo by excluding the extraneous noises of the city or at least her ability to control this:

> Because I haven't got the external sort of noises around me I feel I'm in a bit of a world of my own because I can't really hear so much of what is going on around me. (Mandy: interview number 43)

The use of a personal stereo either creates the experience of being 'cocooned' by separating the user from the outside world or alternatively the user moves outwards into the public realm of communication 'culture' through a private act of reception and becomes absorbed into it. This demonstrates the dialectical nature of personal-stereo use. The user does not perceive herself as being 'alone' but understands that neither is she 'really there'. Using a personal stereo makes her feel more secure as it acts as a kind of 'boundary marker' for her.[1]

Her use of a personal stereo transforms her experience of place and social distance. Through use, the nature and meaning of being 'connected' within a reconfiguration of subject and object itself becomes problematic. The very distinction between them appears to be blurred. The following description of situatedness is typical in which the user describes use as filling:

> The space whilst you're walking . . . It also changes the atmosphere as well. If you listen to music, like, and you're feeling depressed it can change the atmosphere around you. (Sara: interview number 50)

The auditory quality of listening is described as being all engulfing. The site of experience is transformed from the inside out. Effectively it is colonized. Habitable space becomes both auratic and intimate:[2]

> Because when you have the Walkman it's like having company. You don't feel lonely. It's your own environment. It's like you're doing something pleasurable you can do by yourself and enjoy it. I think it creates a sense of kind of aura sort of like. Even though it's directly in your ears you feel like it's all around your head. You're really aware it's just you, only you can hear it. It makes you feel individual . . . Listening also constitutes 'company': If there's the radio there's always somebody talking. There's always something happening. (Alice: interview number 6)

This is contrasted with the observation that nothing is happening if there is no musical accompaniment to experience. The auratic space of habitation collapses. The nature of a world of 'we-ness' is a world accompanied by mediated messages of culture and its social formation in which patterns of habit exist along a gradient that moves in the direction of dependency. When the personal stereo is switched off the 'we-ness' falls away and the user is left in an experiential void often described with various degrees of apprehension or annoyance. Left to themselves with no distractions, users often experience feelings of anxiety. This is apparent in the many users who either put their personal stereos on to go to sleep or alternatively go to sleep with sound or music from their record players or radios. The activity is of course pleasurable in its own right:

> I like something to sing me to sleep. Usually Bob Marley because I don't like silence. It frightens me. If it's silent and it's dark as well. It helps me think. Because I have trouble sleeping so if I have a song I like; it's sort of soothing. It's like your mum rocking you to sleep. I like someone to sing me to sleep. (Jana: interview number 47)

> I don't like silence. I hate it at night. I suppose it's at night and you're on your own. I just don't like being alone. I just have to have someone with me or if not with me some type of noise. That's why I have music on for. It kinds of hides it. It just makes me feel comfortable. (Kim: interview number 25)

> Just having the noise. If it's not music I have the TV. If there's the radio there's always someone talking. There's something happening. (Sara: interview number 50)

These responses contextualize the role of personal stereos to other forms of communication technologies that also act as forms of 'we-ness'. Dorinda, a thirty-year-old mother describes using her personal stereo whilst cycling. For her the state of 'being with' is very specific. She plays one tape for months on end on her personal stereo. At present it is Scott Walker sings Jacques Brel. The tape has personal connotations for her and whilst listening she describes feeling confident, as if she's 'with' the singer. The sense of security she gains from this imagined familiarity is conveyed in the following remark:

> Yeh. It's me and Scott [Walker] on the bike. (Dorinda: interview number 32)

Other users also describe this in terms of a feeling of being protected. Their own space becomes a protected zone where they are 'together' with the content of their personal stereo:

> If I'm in a difficult situation or in new surroundings then I think nothing can affect you, you know. It's your space. (Paul: interview number 45)

Use appears to function as a substitute for company in these examples. Instead of company sound installs itself, usually successfully. Jade, an habitual user describes his relationship with his personal stereo in interpersonal terms in which the machine becomes an extension of his body. Users often describe feeling more comfortable when they touch or are aware of the physical presence of their personal stereo. These users normally don't like other people to use their machine:

> It's a little like another person. You can relate to it. You get something from it. They share the same things as you do. You relate to it as if its another person. Though you can't speak to it. The silence is freaky for me. That is kind of scary. It's almost like a void if you like. (Jade: interview number 13)

The above extract is also indicative of the feeling of being 'deserted' when the music stops. This feeling might also be described in terms of communication technology enhancing the space and the time of the user. As such it becomes both taken for granted and 'everyday' in terms of the user's experience. Experience without it is seen as either void or at least inferior to experience through it. The spacing of experience becomes transformed as the following group of teenagers testify:

> It fills the space whilst you're walking. (Rebecca: interview number 49)

> It also changes the atmosphere as well. If you listen to music you really like and your feeling depressed it can change the atmosphere around you. It livens everything up. (Sara: interview number 50)

The invigoration and heightening of the space of experience enacted through use collapses the distinction between private mood or orientation and the user's surroundings. The world becomes one with the experience of the user as against the threatened disjunction between the two. Using a personal stereo colonizes space for these users, transforming their mood, orientation and the reach (Silverstone 1994) of their experience. The quality of these experiences are dependent upon the continued use of the personal stereo. This is graphically demonstrated by the following seventeen-year-old respondents who were asked in a group interview to describe how the atmosphere changes with the switching off of their personal stereos:

> An empty feeling (Kayz: interview number 54)

Got nothing to do. (Zoe: interview number 53)

Just sitting there and get bored (Donna: interview number 52)

It's like when your in a pub and they stop the music. It's an anticlimax. Everyone just stops. You don't know what to say. (Sara: interview number 50)

Switching off becomes tantamount to killing off their private world and returning them to the diminished space and duration of the disenchanted and mundane outside world. The above appears to represent a world of use that is in itself technologized with the experience, the condition and object of that experience being indistinguishable.

The heightening and colonizing nature of personal-stereo use is clearly brought out in the following examples of holiday use. Personal stereos are a popular holiday companion for users:

I use it lying on the beach. You need music when you're tanning yourself. There's the waves and everybody's around. You just need your music. On the plane we were listening to Enigma and things like that. It fitted in . . . Not bored, it livens everything up. Everything's on a higher level all the time. It makes it seem a bit busier. You get exited. Everything's happening. (Donna: interview number 52)

Donna isn't describing use as an antidote to boredom but as a form of harmonizing the environment to herself. Using a personal stereo 'enhances' her experience helping her to create a 'perfect' environment. Use allows her to experience the environment through her mediated fantasies. The holiday brochure might also come to life through use as Jay's description demonstrates:

I use it on the beach. I feel that I'd be listening to my music. I have the sea, I have the sand. I have the warmth but I don't have all the crap around me. I can eliminate that and I can get much more out of what the ocean has to offer me. I can enjoy. I feel that listening to my music, I can really pull those sun's rays. Not being disturbed by screaming kids and all that shouting which is not why I went there. I went to have harmony with the sea and the sun . . . The plane journey, flying out and back and you listen to different music, but it just helps me to still my mind and to centre myself and I feel that by taking this tape with me

I'm carrying that all day and I feel that I'm able to take more from the day and give more to the day. Whether that's right or wrong I don't know but that's how I feel (Jay: interview number 33)

The environment is re-appropriated and experienced as part of the users desire. Through her privatized auditory experience the listener gets 'more' out of the environment, not by interacting with it but precisely by not interacting. Jay focuses on herself as personally receiving the environment via her personal stereo. There is only the sun and the users body and state of mind.

Actual environments, unadorned, are not normally sufficient for personal-stereo users. It is either populated with people (Jay) or merely mundane (Donna). Music listened to through the personal stereo makes it 'what it is' for the user and permits the recreation of the desired space to accord with the wishes of the user. This is achieved by the user repossessing space as part of, or constitutive of their subjective desire. Personal-stereo users thus tend to colonize and appropriate the here-and-now as part of the re-inscribing of habitable space through the 'colonizing' of place.

Personal-Stereo Use: Home and Auditory Mnemonics

Just as representational space is transformed, so is the user's experience of 'habitable' space. As personal-stereo users traverse the public spaces of the city they often describe the experience in terms of never leaving 'home', understood either symbolically or sometimes literally. The aim here is not to reach outwards into a form of 'we-ness' but rather to negate distance enabling the user to maintain a desired sense of security. Using a personal stereo is often described in terms of a feeling of being surrounded or enveloped. This is what users frequently mean when they refer to feelings of being at 'home'. Only the auditory nature of experience appears to be so all encompassing and non-directional. The use of music that has personal associations or connotations heightens these feelings. Equally personalized music enables the user to recreate a sense of narrative that overlays or re-inscribes journeying in public. This represents an alternative route 'home'. Jay typifies the first point:

I like to have a piece of my own world. Familiar and secure. It's a familiarity. Something you're taking with you from your home. You're not actually leaving home. You're taking it with you. You're in your own little bubble. You're in your own little world and you have a certain amount of control and you don't have so much interruption . . . What it evokes for me is that I didn't really have to worry about it at all because there's someone there who'll take care of me. In a sense like when you're little and you have your mum and dad. so that's what it would evoke for me, a feeling of security that it will be all right . . . I don't like it (the urban) to totally take over. I have to have a piece of my own world (Jay: interview number 33)

Jay listens to tapes that she associates with her own world and memories. She does not visualize this sense of home literally in terms of concrete memories but rather relates to it in terms of a sense of well-being and security. In this sense, she does not demonstrate an interest in an ongoing communicative process with a socially constructed public state of 'we-ness'. Rather, certain tunes or songs give her a heightened sense of well-being reminding her of childhood and family.

Other users describe travelling back into their own narratives by visualizing situations or re-experiencing the sensation of pleasurable situations whilst listening to their personal stereos in discounted public spaces. Their imaginary journey takes precedence over their actual physical journey and their actual 'present' is overridden by their 'imaginary' present. Whilst daydreaming is a common activity, users appear to have great difficulty conjuring up these feelings and images of home and narrative without using their personal stereos. As such, daydreaming becomes mediated, constructed and constituted through the technological medium of personal stereos and music.

The control exerted over the external environment through use is also described in terms of clearing a 'space' for thoughts or the imagination. The random nature of the sounds of the street does not produce the correct configuration or force to successfully produce or create the focusing of thoughts in the desired direction. For users who are habitually accompanied by music there arises a need for accompaniment as a constituent part of their experience. The world and their biography is recollected and accompanied by sound. This construction of a space or clearing for the imagination to, either function in, or be triggered by personal-stereo use appears to be connected to the habitualness of use rather than the type of environment within which the experience takes place. It often makes little difference to the user whether they are walking down a deserted street or travelling on a congested train in terms of the production of the states of 'being' discussed here.

Home and narrative appear to be closely connected in the lifeworld of users. Personal stereos can be construed as functioning as a form of 'auditory mnemonic' in which users attempt to construct a sense of narrative within urban spaces that have no narrative sense for them. The construction of a narrative becomes an attempt to maintain a sense of pleasurable coherence in those spaces that are perceived to be bereft of interest. Users describe a variety of situations relating to this point:

> The music sparks off memories. Just like that. As soon as you hear the tunes. (Kim: interview number 25)

> I'll remember the place. I'll be there. I'll remember what I was doing when I was listening to that music. (Jana: interview number 47)

> If I'm listening to Ben E. King's 'Stand by Me' I can imagine myself walking down Leicester Square because that's where I heard it with that guy. (Mandy: interview number 43)

> I'd visualize it. Like if I heard a certain song at a party or something and when I heard it again on my Walkman I'd just be at that party again with my friends doing what I was doing. (Zoe: interview number 53)

> Sometimes it brings back memories. Like how you felt. Some types of music and songs like, you only listen to them at certain times with certain people, so you listen to them on your own and it brings back memories . . . atmospheres. (Sara: interview number 50)

> Every time you listen to music it takes you back . . . I visualize it. Like if I heard a certain song at a party or something and when I heard it again on my Walkman I'd just be at that party again with my friends doing what I was doing. (Rebecca: interview number 49)

> Certain songs remind you of home, or of situations. The situation seems to stick in my mind. Oh! I was there when I listened to that. (Paul: interview number 37)

> Especially here, where I don't have such a big network of social connections. It's like [listening to music on his Walkman] having a photo of old friends. (Magnus: interview number 21)

Personal stereo use therefore represents one form of biographical travelling. The narrative quality that users attach to music permits them to reconstruct these narrative memories at will in places where they would otherwise have difficulty in summoning them up. These memories provide the user with a feeling of being wrapped up in their own significance whilst existing in the perceived narrative anonymity or invisibility of their spatial present. Sound appears as the significant medium here as users rarely describe constructing narratives out of television-watching for example, at least whilst alone and in public areas.

Place as Body in Personal-Stereo Use

The use of personal stereos also helps users to reconceptualize their experience of the body as the 'site' of action. The relationship of sound to the body also demonstrates the dual nature of the auditory. It is both a 'distance' sense as is sight, as well as a 'contact' sense together with touch and taste. The physicality of sound is brought out admirably by the following user's description:

> You hear things not just through your eardrums, but through your whole bones. Your whole body is vibrating. I suppose it cancels out the vibration from the traffic around you. (Karin: interview number 18)

Users often describe feelings of being energized. The following account of cycling to the sounds of the personal stereo is typical:

> It's like when you've got music on and you're on your bike. It's like flying in a way. You're kind of away from things and you're not having any other contact with people. So flying above everything I suppose. You're more aware of cycling. Of the physical action of cycling. (Dorinda: interview number 32)

The experience of cycling is thus transformed. A heightened sense of the body as the site of action is commonly described by users, especially those who use them for physical activity. This type of use often results in an 'emptying out' of thoughts from the body together with a greater awareness of the body as the 'site' of action:

> I'd enjoy the feeling of my body working hard. It made me more concentrated on that. I enjoyed the feeling. It was channelling you in on that feeling. I'm used to riding a bike as well. Riding the push bike for the same reason. Focusing inside. Getting in a rhythm. Certain tracks, get into a rhythm, follow the bass line. It's always dance music. It's got

energy. It's like clubbing or dancing. I get the same energy working or cycling. You become part of the bicycle. (Ben: interview number 4)

In these descriptions the physical body becomes the centre of action. This can be understood as a form of 'de-consciousnessing' by which I mean the giving over of oneself to the body as the site of 'action'. The closest analogy would be the experience of extended dancing at 'rave' evenings (Malbon 1998). Dorinda's account differs from Ben's, however, because whilst the body becomes a site of action, she is not alone. She is in the company of the tape and 'Scott Walker'. Whereas in Ben's account he is focusing in on the rhythm and is at one with that. In both accounts, however, the body is experienced as merging with the activity of cycling. As such the body tends to lose its weight and resistance, becoming consumed in the present thus banishing time. For users to successfully produce this experience the personal stereo must normally be played loudly in order to preclude the intrusive sounds of the world that would otherwise threaten to diminish the experience. Users are often aware of the possibility of sound encroaching into their world and respond by varying the sound level of their personal stereo appropriately, thus maintaining the hermetically sealed nature of their listening experiences.

Users' relations to representational space are transformed, enabling them to construct forms of 'habitable' space for themselves. In doing so users can be described as creating a fragile world of certainty within a contingent world. Users tend not to like being left to their own thoughts, not for them the reveries of a Rousseau who liked nothing more than walking in the solitude of the countryside in order to be alone with his own thoughts. Personal-stereo users prefer to be 'alone' with the mediated sounds of the culture industry. Users thus become empowered, paradoxically, over themselves. I discuss this in detail in the following chapter.

Notes

1. Goffman states that a boundary marker:

   marks the line between two adjacent territories. Note when boundary markers
   are employed either on both sides of an individual or in front and back, they

function as 'spacers' ensuring the user personal space in a row or column. (Goffman 1971, p. 66)

2. Benjamin defines aura as 'A strange weave of space and time: the unique semblance of distance, no matter how close the object may be' (1973b, p. 250). For Howard Caygill:

> Aura is not a property but rather an effect of a particular mode of transmitting a work of art, one which privileges its originality and uniqueness. Aura is not the predicate of a work of art but a condition, now surpassed, of its transmission. As a condition it has a cultural significance beyond the sphere of art, indeed aura describes a particular form of experience appropriate to a particular culture and stage of technological development. (Caygill 1998, p. 112–13)

Personal Stereos and the Management of Cognitive Contingency

[There is] an unimaginable closeness of sound technology and self awareness, a simulacrum of a feedback loop relaying sender to receiver. A song sings to a listening ear, telling it to sing. As if the music were originating in the brain itself, rather than emanating from stereo speakers or headphones.

F. Kittler, *Gramophone, Film and Typewriter*

If personal-stereo users make technologically mediated sanctuaries out of much of their experience how then do they manage these sanctuaries? In the following pages I demonstrate users as being extremely sensitive to the contingent nature of their own cognitive processes, their thoughts and emotions. Personal stereos are used effectively to extend the range of management that users have over a wide range of personal experience. Users demonstrate little of the postmodern desire for decentredness commonly found in the literature on contemporary experience. Rather, theirs is a lifeworld filled with potential anxiety concerning the threat of decentredness within a world of contingency in which the technologizing of experience becomes a successful antidote. Personal-stereo use enables the user to transform both their relationship to themselves and the world beyond them. It is precisely this management of internal contingency which I focus upon in the following pages. In doing so I demonstrate how personal stereos are used as strategic devices in managing and changing the relationship between thought, emotion and volition. Personal-stereo use mediates and in so doing changes the dynamic between intention, thought and the subsequent orientation of the user to their experience. The perceived contingency of their everyday experience is reduced through the enhanced predictability of their experience engendered through personal-stereo use. The mobility of the personal stereo permits users to manage their experience over a vastly greater area of everyday life than was previously possible. I divide these management strategies into two broad areas: firstly, I discuss the way in which personal-stereo users create and maintain moods and feelings through use and, secondly, I investigate users' strategies aimed at controlling their thoughts.

Creating and Maintaining Mood and Feeling

The lifeworld of personal-stereo users is constructed and bounded through the reorganizing of their relationship to both the 'space' within which their thoughts and intentions arise and the field or social horizon within which they are physically situated. In doing so, personal-stereo use both clarifies and simplifies their relationship to these areas of experience, giving users greater control over mood, feeling and thought. This maintenance of control can take a variety of forms. The following user achieves it through recycling time by repeatedly playing the same music on his personal stereo:

> If I'm in a bad mood then I'll get my Walkman. I've got this Living Colour, this heavy rock and I'll play that . . . I think I try to sustain a mood that I'm in, a good mood, by forwarding. The song that I come in, when I wake up in the morning. The first song I hear on the radio is the song that will go in my mind the whole day. So I play my Walkman and try to get rid of that song. I'll play my favourite song in the morning of the tape that I'm listening to and then I suppose I keep forwarding, rewinding it. I've a couple of tapes where I've recorded the same song twice so I don't have to keep rewinding it. I try to sustain the mood. If you're on a plateau. If I go into a shop like Next you want to remain on that plateau. In that good mood until you get there. I've got it on and I'm going through a crowd of people. They're just like hurdles. You try to get past them as quick as possible to make sure, the people, the crowd, don't get into your world so to speak. Mess up your state of mind. (Jade: interview number 13)

The random nature of experience is thus overlaid by the act of listening in which a conscious attempt to replace the sounds of public space with the user's own sound world is enacted. The user repeatedly plays his or her own favourite track of 'the tape of the day' so as to sustain the chosen mood. The same favourite or 'successful' track will be multiply recorded onto the tape and played continuously. This not a too infrequent activity amongst those users who wish to maintain a static mood whilst being physically mobile. In the above example the mood is sustained through a series of complex social manoeuvres. The external environment is perceived as an obstacle to be surmounted. The context of the user's experience is thus perceived to be unnecessary but potentially intrusive and thus destructive to the user's ability to maintain states of control. Mood maintenance and experiencing the 'public' unadorned is seen as mutually exclusive to this user. Auditory distance is needed in order to successfully accomplish strategies of mood maintenance.

Users frequently mention feelings of calm, gained through listening to personal stereos, in which the street is often represented as a mere backcloth, having minimal significance to the user. Personal-stereo use functions to simplify the users environment thus enabling users to focus more clearly on their own state of being precisely by minimizing the contingency of the street. The focusing upon mood and the directing of intention often begins for the user at the start of the day:

> I tend to listen to music that makes me happy. I can put on music and immediately I'll feel much lighter and more with it. It gives me more energy. (Julie: interview number 12)

Users frequently attempt to control their mood or activity through listening to music as demonstrated by the following users:

> I was listening to that as I was getting ready in the house and so I took it out of the tape in the house and put it in my Walkman. It kept me in the mood I was in. (Catherine: interview number 3)

> I find that music is a very personal thing and I mean especially on a Walkman. You're taking all the ones you really like and all the personal tracks. Putting it on a disc tape and listening to it out of choice on your Walkman. So I think that that the music you listen to on a Walkman is more personal than that which you listen to at home. (Ed: interview number 59)

> It sort of wakes you up and you're like; I can do anything now. It kind of makes you energetic. (Jemma: interview number 1)

> If you've got a Walkman it definitely wakes you up. If I'm listening to happy music it puts me in a good mood. It's definitely preparing you for the day. (Paul: interview number 45)

The above descriptions of use might be described as simultaneously active and passive with users describing personal-stereo use as both acting on them and as being instrumentally used by them. Prominent amongst their descriptions is the aim of mood maintenance coupled with the desire to be in, and remain in, a particular frame of mind once it is chosen. Personal-stereo use enables them to achieve this aim. Once out in the street the strategy of mood maintenance, often begun in the home, is extended into the public realm. There are a variety of ways in which this process is undertaken. For example the following user mobilizes his personal stereo in order to change his 'depressed' mood:

> I put on Two Unlimited or *The Magic Flute* by Mozart or maybe Tchaikovsky's Violin Concerto. It will be 99 per cent likely to get me in a better mood again. Yesterday I was really tired. I needed something with a beat. So I have four or five of these tapes with mixed hits. I took one of them that I hadn't listened to for a while. When I have this it's more like going to a club or an aerobics class. That's the kind of thing I like to do. Doing these things gives me energy. The beat. To get me going. Then after a while I'm O.K. If I'm really angry with something. If I listen to music it helps me stress out. It helps me. It stops background noise. I can concentrate on my thoughts. (Magnus: interview number 21)

Users often describe the transformative function of listening to music through personal stereos in terms of 'energy'. Use is described as kick-starting them into the required mood often through concentrated listening. The urban space inhabited by Magnus is seen, as in previous examples, as 'background noise' that represents a presence that threatens to hinder the aim of concentration on his own thoughts. Without the 'background noise' of the world, 'space' is created in his head enabling alternative thoughts to take place.

Mood enhancement is also a very common feature of use, as the following example illustrates:

> If I'm in a bad mood I listen to different sorts of music. I turn it up louder. I don't want anyone else to put me in a bad mood. If I'm in a bad mood I have to block everything out so nobody else can put me in a

bad mood. If I'm in an O.K. mood it puts me in an even better mood. But it won't get me out of a bad mood. (Gemma: interview number 24)

Personal stereo use in this example acts to both insulate the user from the contingency of the outside and to confirm and enhance her mood. Mood is enhanced by increasing the volume such that 'headspace' is dramatically saturated. Through a process of hermetic sealing, even a 'bad' mood can be vicariously enjoyed in that she believes that nothing else can destabilize her. This user, unlike the previous example, claims that use will not change her mood but merely act to enhance whatever mood she's already in. This indicates that the effect of personal stereo listening on the mood of the user is mediated through the volition or character of the user and is thus a dependent variable, albeit a very powerful one in mood management. However, whatever mood the user may be in, greater pleasure is derived from that mood through personal-stereo use as it is experienced with greater intensity:

I really like miserable songs. I like the one's where. You know. They're really heart broken. It's quite nice to sing along to them. I've actually got a problem about travelling and so I try to get all these ways of making it more interesting. I might put Matilda on to feel sort of more bouncy. But I wouldn't put it on to cheer me up. I'm more likely to put it on to heighten my depression. It's quite positive, even though it's depressing stuff. I like that kind of stuff. So it's fun. (Dorinda: interview number 32)

Typically this user enjoys her depressive or melancholic moods more if she can enhance them by listening to music. By taking her mood out with her, stabilized and enhanced to music, she is able to 'experience' her mood and enjoy it in public. Without this stimulus the 'aestheticization' of her mood would not be so pleasurable or successful. Once again it appears that the pleasure derived is directly proportional to an increased focus on subjective mood and a decreased or sublimated experience of the public realm. The following example is typical of mood maintenance continued from the users home to the outside environment:

I do have it on loud sometimes if I'm going out and I'm enjoying something I'll take it with me and that is the start of, bringing something from the house to take with me to go where I'm going. The music in the house is a mood enhancer and then I wish to take it with me . . . It can change it [mood]. It can make me. Those going to work things particularly. I'd say that if I'm going out for an evening it would block, or it would keep it. Preserve it. But actually going to work can change it. Particularly if otherwise I'm going to think. I bet so and so hasn't done this. It can help me arrive much sweeter with much more level expectations. (Betty: interview number 34)

This continuation of mood from home to street is achieved by bridging these spaces with music. In doing so, the distance from leaving her house to arriving at her destination is negated or overlaid by the use of her personal stereo. Her mood is orientated to the expectation of her arrival and this is achieved or preserved by a process of blocking out all exteriority. However these responses are also mediated by specific circumstances. If, for example, a user is merely going to work, then use might change their mood into one that is more suitable, successful and appropriate for the tasks of the day. This is achieved by using the personal stereo to deflect thoughts from any problematic futures thereby precluding the creation of any possible tension. Use can be described as creating a 'space' within which users unwind and unravel their emotions, thus providing a base for thinking clearly or lucidly:

I'll be listening to something in my room on the radio. I'll say. Oh! I love this tune. I'll continue this on my Walkman. If I'm feeling quite lively, full of energy, then I'll put on something upbeat. If I'm feeling tired. Something acoustic. It relaxes you. If you're stressed out you can't concentrate and you put something on and you forget for a little while. You can think clearly about what you actually need to do because you've had a little bit of time to unwind. (Mags: interview number 31)

The use of a personal stereo as a mood maintainer or mood transformer can work in a variety of directions allowing the user to relax or to enhance their emotions. Use also permits the user to focus upon music so as to deflect or recess thoughts and moods that might otherwise be experienced as unpleasant or uncontrollable:

Sometimes I'm really angry. I get annoyed. I might be quite ratty and then I'll get quite aggressive. So I'd use quite fast music. Sometimes it calms me down and I have to listen to something else but sometimes I'll just have to keep listening to it all day. I'll just be in that mood all day. (Sarah: interview number 27)

I argue a lot with my parents. When I go out of the house it calms me down. It starts the day off better. It helps to keep me in the clouds. It's quite happy music. So that helps me quite a lot. It calms me down. I know all the words. Because I know something, I can concentrate on that. My thoughts are more structured when I have my Walkman. It's more positive. (Kim: interview number 25)

Personal-stereo use enables users to cope with, or deal with, stressful emotional situations through use in situations when they would otherwise feel vulnerable, alone or when they feel they would otherwise be forced to think about unwanted things due to a lack of distraction. Personal stereos become tools of distraction in these instances by removing users' unwanted thoughts. These examples indicate that personal-stereo users are at their most vulnerable, in terms of the vicissitudes of their own mind, when they are alone in public spaces. Personal stereos appear to act as a prop against this tendency:

Ten years ago there was a lot going on with me and the Walkman very much – acted like an escape. You know. Getting away from it all. Being sort of transported somewhere else for a while. So yeh. It was definitely a bit of escapism. It alleviated a lot of stuff. My parents had divorced. My mother was experiencing a pretty traumatic breakdown at the time. So it was nice to be anywhere. Music made me happy. If I didn't have the Walkman I'd feel what was going on around me. (Betty: interview number 34)

Unwanted thoughts are blocked out during her journeying till she arrives at her destination where her attention is taken up with other things. In this instance the personal stereo functions as a kind of 'in-between', filling up time and space in between contact with others, transporting the user out of place and time into a form of weightlessness of the present. Personal-stereo use thus becomes a source of mental clearing for many users. Personal-stereo use appears to create a mental space for users enabling them to 'rest' there successfully:

It kind of helped me think in perspective. It helped me think things through. It takes the situation out of the immediate surroundings. You're just somewhere else so you can think about things. (Amber: interview number 28)

This user describes being 'taken out' of her situation enabling her to think more clearly and permitting her to 'get away' from any nagging thoughts or worries that threaten to intrude on her. It is as if the burden of thought that threatens to drag her down dissipates through use. Personal stereos, by excluding the outside, permit users to structure their 'insides' and create a 'free', 'orderly' and 'mobile' space for themselves. Users describe striving to 'free' themselves from their own thoughts so as to be able to channel themselves into whatever they might physically be doing. The following user describes using a personal stereo whilst working on a motorway:

> There's a lot of empty spaces in your head. Too much time to dwell on your everyday problems [at work] . . . It [Walkman use] distracted you from what you were doing but it helped you with what you were doing. (Ben: interview number 41)

When the confusion of the world intrudes, users invariably describe running for their personal stereo.

Controlling and Excluding Thoughts

What if the potential chaos resides in the mind of the user? Personal-stereo use enables users to manage the intrusive nature of their own thoughts successfully. The proximity of an amplified auditory resounding through the heads of users enables them to construct successful evasive strategies over their own unwanted thought processes:

> I don't think about my feelings. I just shut everything out. That's why I play the music really loud. I'll just listen to the music and blank everything out. (Mary: interview number 5)

> There were no real thoughts. It squashed thoughts. I suppose I didn't like being alone with my thoughts. I had a feeling I knew what they were going to be. (Chris: interview number 11)

> If you've got a problem you don't have to really think about it. (Joseph: interview number 55)

> I only listen to my Walkman because I need to have sound constantly. I need to be listening to something otherwise it will make you think about other things that you don't really want to think about. (Isobel: interview number 26)

> Sometimes it helps me not to think. I just sit there and listen. Sometimes you're walking. You're listening and thinking at the same time. If I'm in a bad mood I listen to punk music. (John: interview number 20)

This blotting out of thoughts is described as being achieved relatively easily through use. The user merely increases the volume and concentrates on the resonating sounds coming through their personal stereos. The immediacy and volume of the sound ensures success. Users invariably describe these experiences as all-encompassing in their physical directness and power. The random nature of the sounds of the street, no matter how loud or chaotic, are unable to produce the correct configuration or force to successfully permit the user to do this. Listening provides a technological method of allowing the user not to be alone with their thoughts. This forgetting of 'self' has a variety of meanings within personal stereo use and need not be total. The following example is of a woman going to work who doesn't wish to think about whether she's feeling particularly 'good' or not. In this instance thought is held in suspension:

> Maybe it stops me from wondering how I feel. It gives me something else to be in there that isn't wondering how I feel or what I'm going to say. It keeps me in myself. (Jo: interview number 30)

The use of a personal stereo also provides the opportunity for not thinking about specific concerns. The personal stereo acts as a temporary distraction until users come into contact with others or reach their destination when alternative distractions beckon. Users often describe use in terms of being taken 'out of themselves'. Feelings of distress are transformed, at least temporarily, into feelings of pleasure through attending to the sounds of their personal stereos. Users describe these experiences in terms of being 'transported somewhere else'. The following user listens compulsively to her personal stereo:

> I listen to some piece of music for a long time. The thoughts come back and I have to change the tape. (Isobel: interview number 26)

The compulsive nature of listening to the same piece of music enables her both to maintain her mood and to exclude alternative, unwanted, thought. Used in this way the piece of music appears to have slowly diminishing returns. This is not the same for those users who habitually use the same piece of music to enhance experiences or use music to give them a feeling of security. Music can also direct thoughts into specific and desired directions. Music, as noted in the previous chapter, provides a powerful sense of personal narrative for many users. Specific songs will often evoke specific thoughts relating to the listener's biography. This is one reason why users derive such pleasure by immersing themselves in music. The following user describes this process in terms of colonization or engulfment:

> The music is not like a background. It's all around you. It takes over your senses. It can be quite isolating. (Karen: interview number 18)

This sense of isolation, of being 'cocooned' away from the world is also apparent in the following quote from Mags who is an intermittent user. She describes absenting herself from her situation on the tube whilst returning from work rather than escaping from unwanted thoughts. She doesn't want to think but merely relax in her state of tiredness:

> It's background. It's something to drown out the noise of the train. If you want to switch off and be in a room of your own you put that on and you close your eyes and shut your ears and it's a way of not being bothered. (Mags: interview number 31)

The use of a personal stereo 'drowns out' geographical space and places her 'into a room of her own' by 'closing her ears and shutting her eyes' to the space occupied but not inhabited. Users like Mags describe certain personal- stereo 'states' as enclosing. This represents a shutting off of the senses from their physical environment so as to 'drift off' within their own hermetically sealed space. Users can, however, continually transform their orientation to themselves and the world.

Yet any attempt to recreate phenomenologically users' experience of 'duree' is fraught with problems of hypostasization and reification as the following user's account illustrates:

> The music leads you to something and then you go back to the music. It leads me to different thoughts. Sometimes it gives me other ways. Other directions for my thoughts but it doesn't change my mood. I feel stronger. Not because I've got the music. If I feel stronger it's because the music gives, like, a frame for my thoughts and with my thoughts I feel stronger. It's not the music because anybody else can have the same tape on the Walkman but not my thoughts. Sometimes I like not to think at all. I just listen to the music and feel good the same. I just follow the music. Just concentrate on the music. (Claudia: interview number 38)

This description captures the fleeting and complex set of experiences framed through personal-stereo use that are both active and passive.

The user interacts with the music on the personal stereo in order to direct her thoughts towards an open-ended imaginary thought process but also blanks thoughts out altogether. This example also clearly demonstrates how analytically unhelpful it is to distinguish between different types of user rather than different types of use.

Personal-stereo users demonstrate a heightened sense of the contingent nature of their everyday experience, which they manage through the use of their personal stereos. This chapter has demonstrated the strategies users operationalize in their attempts to string together and control the disparate nature of their everyday experience through the technologization of their experience. These strategies become habitual, dependent and sedimented into users' everyday experience.

The Re-appropriation of Time in Everyday Life

But one could no more imagine Nietzsche in an office, with a secretary minding the telephone in an anteroom, at his desk until five o'clock, then playing golf after the day's work was done.

T. Adorno, *Minima Moralia: Reflections from Damaged Life*

The public sense of time and space is frequently contested within the social order. This in part arises out of individual and subjective resistance to the absolute authority of the clock and the tyranny of the cadastral map.

D. Harvey, *Justice, Nature and the Geography of Difference*

Each morning when we confront a familiar world. Considering the day ahead we mark off that which might be pleasurable from that which will produce anxiety, irritation, boredom and depression.

S. Cohen and L. Taylor, *Escape Attempts*

Time is the dominant contingency of everyday life. How, then, do personal-stereo users manage time? As they awake each morning to face the day ahead they invariably are not alone, their day normally begins accompanied by the radio, television or the sound system. The beginning of the day with its domestic routines is constituted through 'being with' the products of these artifacts of the culture industry. Preparation time for the day, rather than being experienced as 'empty' is rather filled. Personal-stereo use enables them to continue to manage segments of their daily routine as they leave home. In the street users demonstrate an attentiveness to the daily management of their time consonant to their desire to manage other areas of their daily life illustrated in earlier chapters. In this chapter I chart users' time-management strategies as they face the repetitive nature of their daily routines.

> I'm a very 'county' person. I look at my watch a lot. When I'm waiting for things or when I'm on the train and like, I'm going to think; 'There'll be three songs till I get to the next station' or I won't look at my watch till I get to West Hampstead. (Mandy: interview number 43)

> What I'll do. When I get on the bus I put my tape on. Three songs before the song that's my favourite that I like to listen to the most. So by the time I get to the bus stop and I've actually started my journey on the bus I'll be listening to that song and I'll be in that mood. (Jade: interview number 13)

Users can either package time into segments, moving towards the journeys end, or concentrate on mood maintenance that overcomes the journey time. Users sometimes record the same piece repeatedly onto the same tape or repeatedly rewind to listen to the same piece in order to achieve this level of time suspension:

> It was just the same one and I listened to it over and over again. It was really nice listening to something over and over again. (Amber: interview number 28)

Time is transcended as the user maintains the mood within the flow of linear time.[1] Users also endow time with their own meaning as they transform their mundane journey time into something more meaningful. The journey itself might become transformed into a form of leisure:

> I'm on the go all the time now and I need music to relax. On the way to work, when I cycle. That's my leisure time. (Stephanie: interview number 42)

> I listen to it [on the tube] because I can't listen at work. Otherwise half an hour of your journey goes. Otherwise I'm wasting an hour of my time doing absolutely nothing ... It relaxes you. If you're stressed or you can't concentrate and you put something on and you can forget for a little while. You can think clearly about what you actually need to do because you've had that time to unwind. (Mags: interview number 31)

Users have both the desire and the required facility to transcend the mundane nature of their everyday routines. Users appear to be resisting the mundane nature of the everyday through personal-stereo use. The management of their experience enables them to negotiate the pitfalls of their 'eversame' with great success. In order to articulate this fully, I draw on three detailed case studies which demonstrates the variety of ways in which cyclical time (which dominates nature, the day, month, the seasons) and linear time (the social organization of the day) is transformed through the use of personal stereos.

Three Case Studies

Example One

Des (interview number 57) is a black, 27-year-old male. He has worked as a scientific technician for the last ten years in the same establishment. He began using personal stereos in 1980, the year they became more widely available in Britain. Des has used his personal stereo regularly ever since. The use is primarily for journeying whilst alone. He is an avid music listener and sees himself as a specialist, especially in the field of Soul Music. His music collection totals over seven thousand discs. He also has state-of-the-art record equipment and two personal stereos, one for CDs and one for tapes, and wears top-of-the-range headphones that wrap around the head. He spends most of his spare money on music saying that 'music is my life to tell you the truth'. He uses his personal stereo exclusively to go to and from work. He doesn't use it at weekends or during his 'leisure' time. He also listens to music all day in the work lab, but not on his personal stereo. The journey that Des makes every day to work remains the same, taking him over an hour each way. He uses his personal stereo 'every day without fail', putting it on as he leaves the door of his house. He uses tapes that he has compiled from his own collection of discs, changing the tapes when appropriate:

> It depends how I'm feeling. I might play a lot of old soul music on a journey because that will fit in.

Listening tends to put him 'in the right frame of mind' for work. To get him in this frame of mind though, he needs to listen and concentrate on the music uninterruptedly. To do this successfully he takes a longer than necessary route to work. The time of the journey is transformed from one of mundaneness and repetitiveness to one reclaimed or repossessed as pleasurable:

> The thing is, I always take the bus to work. I could take the tube but it would be too quick for me. So I like to have at least an hour to get to work and listen to music.

Like many users he is intensely involved in the music:

> I'm into myself. I'm listening to the music. I'm listening to every note. Everything. Because the journey's the same it does get a bit boring. It's the same people on the bus. So I try to block that out of my mind and concentrate. I can't stand being on a bus without a Walkman with a lot of people talking and you're hearing lots of conversations.

This is one method of imposing an alternative routine over mundane linear time. The reinscription invests or overlays a subjectively more satisfying mode of time for the user. The journey is described as both mundane and unpleasant:

> Around that area, Knightsbridge and Chelsea, you get a lot of traffic jams. So I don't want to be without a headset in a traffic jam because I don't buy a newspaper or things like that. So I'd get bored.

Encroaching boredom is allayed by the variety of tapes carried. If one tape doesn't work for him:

> There's another tape that I might not have listened to for a few weeks. So I'll bring that tape out. By the weekend I'll make up a new tape.

The contingency of his journey is thereby minimized. The use of a personal stereo enables him to re-appropriate time. The journey time would otherwise be seen as a form of theft of time whereas using a personal stereo transforms it to an experience of freedom, becoming a pleasurable mood-enhancing activity. This repossession of time is inscribed not merely into journey time but in the various forms of preparation for the journey, such as the making and choosing of the music to be listened to. By engaging in these preparations he suspends the day ahead:

It's just the music. I don't really think about the day ahead much. I try
not to anyway.

Time is clawed back and its possession appears to be significant. Time
possessed need not pass by more quickly. For Des, as with other users,
identity fuses with the music listened to. His music collection assumes
the status of personal identity. In going to and from work he is 'taking
[his] collection with [him]'. Des lives his music whilst in public as a
sign of ownership of that time and space.

Without the personal stereo the idea of the journey and work would
become intolerable. He states that 'I've got to have the headset to get
me in the right frame of mind.' The public space in which use takes
place is perceived as secondary to, and a potential hindrance to, his
experience engendered through his use of a personal stereo. In this
instance Des doesn't use it to block out thoughts about himself or the
day ahead, but rather re-appropriates his time through transforming it
into pleasurable activity. I interpret this as a re-inscribing of mundane
linear time (engaging in the routine activities of life) with his own
form of linear time repeated every workday but in a form chosen by
himself. Des, unlike many younger users, doesn't fill his living space
and time with other products of the culture industry. Silence is not a
problem for him and neither is going out in public without a personal
stereo. The fact that the personal stereo is not used at other times is
instructive in as much as it demonstrates quite clearly the distinction
between freely chosen activity and routine activity. Activities freely
chosen do not require personal stereo accompaniment precisely because
they already 'belong' to the user. The personal stereo thus becomes a
very effective tool for re-appropriating time, as it is in providing
stimulus to the imagination or fantasy of the user in other contexts.

Example Two

Sue (interview number 61) is a 27-year-old secretary and mother who
has regularly used a personal stereo since she was twelve years old. She
wears it both to preclude unwanted social interaction and to claw back
time for herself in her busy daily schedule of work, childcare and home
life.

Well I like listening to music anyway and because I work and because
I've got a child I don't really have time to listen enough to music. So in
order to fit the listening in the Walkman's really good because you can

listen to your Walkman on the way to work or on your way to pick Joe up from the school.

Sue can only snatch at times that she can call her own. This is not to say that she is unhappy with the demands made upon her. Merely that some 'time' and 'space' is considered necessary for her in order to be able to manage her life to her liking. Time reclaimed is perceived by her as time 'stolen'. 'Free time' becomes 'time for herself'.

So I like listening to music and I don't really have any free time for myself.

Forms of activity associated with her normal routines are not defined as either satisfying or 'free'. Shopping, for example, is not 'her' time unless done in conjunction with her use of a personal stereo:

If I'm in a supermarket I have my Walkman on. I don't think I could walk round a supermarket any other way. Supermarket music is always really bad and I just think. 'Damn. I don't want to waste time listening to this music.' I could have found a bit of time for myself.

The activity of shopping becomes 'free time' only in conjunction with listening to 'her' music. Shopping time becomes an occasion where she can steal free time through music use. Equally, merely listening to music doesn't constitute 'free time' for her as she describes having music on all the time whilst at home with her family. The music that she listens to at home is collectively agreed upon and thus isn't necessarily 'her' music. She also has personal music that she prefers to listen to on her own:

Because music is more personal. Listening to it at home? I wouldn't. It wouldn't get me thinking.

In her 'own' time, Sue describes daydreaming to narratives either associated with or suggested by the music. She becomes engrossed in the act of listening and daydreaming. On her way to work she, like Des, describes purposively lengthening her journey time:

If it's a really good track I tend to walk around the building and go through the longest possible route so that I can finish the track before I get into the office.

She does this not because she necessarily dislikes her work but rather in order to get as much out of her uninterrupted personal stereo experience as possible. However, at times when she is bored at work:

> If it's a new tape and it's really dull at work I might just take an hour out and go and listen to some music and have a walk around town.

Time reclaimed for Sue is solitary time. But solitary time becomes enjoyable only through listening to her chosen music. Her own time is time not shared:

> With the Walkman you don't have to share the music with anyone else.

Just as she has favourite music Sue also has favourite books, which she listens to on tapes. Just as with music, these books often represent an escape into her own time. This example also demonstrates that states of 'we-ness' are not only located in the sounds of music but in other forms of mechanized auditory sounds. Sue plays the book tapes on her personal stereo whilst walking:

> If I'm going to the Peak District I normally find time to take a longer walk on my own and Wuthering Heights is just perfect. Because I know the books very well. I know the different scenes and I know exactly how each scene 's going to look. If I'm in the Yorkshire Dales then it's Jane Eyre. It fits the book.

Repeating experience through repeated listening is another way in which both cyclical time (the hours of the day) and linear time are transformed by users:

> When I play CDs that I really like I play them again and again and again and whatever's going on in my life then is related to the music . . . I tend to have one tape (in the Walkman) and I listen to it and listen to it. I play it to death and then go on to the next one.

In doing this she daydreams or constructs an imaginary state which takes her 'somewhere else'. This 'somewhere else' is outside of cyclical and linear time. It becomes her 'compensatory metaphysics'.[2]

Example Three

Chris (interview number 11) is a 34-year-old researcher who works for a consultancy firm in the City of London. His use of a personal stereo can be understood clearly as a reaction to feelings of being trapped in daily and unpleasant work. He first began using a personal stereo to go to and from work when he was twenty-five years old. He also describes using it at work to snatch moments of free time which functions as either a relaxant or as a recharger of energy:

> I was in an area that wasn't carefully monitored. It was all people of my age who hated it [work], so they didn't mind if you sat for a minute and listened to a song or two. I used it as a break from work.

Chris describes disliking the job he was doing at that time. Using a personal stereo helped him to cope with the daily feelings of frustration and unhappiness:

> When I first started work I really hated my job and I used to wear it quite aggressively, putting it on before I unlocked the front door and not turning it off until I was at my desk and at the last possible moment. The idea was I hated the thought of going to work. Also there's a lot of noise and announcements that doesn't have any relationship to what you're doing and the journey you're taking and you don't have to listen to them. You don't have to listen to other people's conversations.

Chris attempts to reclaim as much of his time as possible. This is coupled with an attendant attitude of public disavowal. The use of a personal stereo appears to represents a form of solipsistic obsession with control through the reclaiming of time. All else appears to represent an irrelevant obstacle to his attempt at temporary escape. The obsessive quality of this is demonstrated in his heightened sense of control over his journey time:

> I used to listen to the same tape over and over again on the way to work because the Walkman had a repeat and it would go on as a continuous loop. It got to the point where I could time where I would be by the music.

Lacking any control over his circumstances he simulates an attempted total control over his perception of his journey time by the minute control of music and place. In doing this he manages to block out any thoughts of his destination and the day ahead. He describes retreating into himself by blocking out both the environment and destination through personal-stereo use. The journey itself becomes a function of the sequence of music listened to on the personal stereo. The music, like the journey, remains obsessively the same on each day:

> Most of the music I chose was very evocative of something and I associated it with a particular part of my journey. It became a way of describing that this part of the journey is bearable. You can get through this part. I remember there was a big escalator change at Green Park and I thought 'Right! If I don't have that particular music for that, then I'll fast forward it to get to that and then I can go up.' Like that it made it easier not to let work encroach onto non-work time. It was a way of not allowing thoughts like I've got that deadline and a meeting with so and so. Because the journey to work was so uniform and intrusive.

Chris' reclaiming of time differs somewhat from the earlier examples, especially in its intensity. For Chris, the sense of frustration and impotency with his everyday means that the journey time is merely a prelude to an unpleasant 'everyday'. It is not so much the mundane features of the journey which is at issue but the nature of work perceived as a form of inevitable theft. Whilst work time cannot be controlled, journey time can through a form of compulsive repetition and fantasy of control. Thoughts are described as being cast out whereas in the first example, the routine of work is not perceived as being especially unpleasant, especially as the user can play music continuously through-out the day. In the previous examples the personal stereo isn't used primarily as a form of thought eradication but as a form of reclaiming journey time through pleasurable activity. Alternatively it represented the creation of 'private' time in which an imaginary present was created. Chris, however, explains the function of the personal stereo for him at that time in the following way:

> It blocks out and certainly alters reality. You're not fully there. I think that's why I was so frustrated about not having the right piece of music and if I just had a classical tape and I couldn't block everything out that was the most frustrating.

External intrusion thus breaks the bubble of control and ruins the imaginary flight into sound and rhythm. In order to 'block out' the journey and the thought of the destination the journey is scripted to the last minute detail. The same music is played each day facilitating minute control of each part of the journey. In this way the acute alienation that Chris feels towards his daily routine is alleviated through the use of his personal stereo.

Repossessing Time

The above examples demonstrate that the use of personal stereos enables users to successfully repossess time. The repressive nature of industrialized time has been frequently commented upon and the analysis of personal-stereo use sheds considerable light on the daily experience of urban time. Adorno pointed to the fragmentation of time in the everyday life of urban dwellers together with the ambiguous role played by leisure in the make up of everyday life:

> Atomisation is advancing not only between men, but within each individual, between the spheres of his life. No fulfilment may be attached to work, which would otherwise lose its functional modesty in the totality of purposes, no spark of reflection is allowed to fall into leisure time, since it might otherwise leap across to the workaday world and set it on fire. While in their structure work and amusement are becoming increasingly alike, they are at the same time being divided ever more rigorously by invisible demarcation lines. (Adorno 1974, p. 130)

Personal-stereo use can be interpreted as a way of reconstituting or obscuring the notion of private atomization. Users appear to rejoin disparate areas of their private life such that journey time, perceived to hold little meaning other than merely constituting the realm of the 'eversame', is overridden by appropriating time precisely through the products of the culture industry. Users may or may not like their jobs, but they invariably do not like their public journeys or time spent alone. Users also often describe attempts to reclaim part of their work time. By playing a personal stereo at work an office cleaner might make work more pleasurable. Workers listen whilst working at their computers, to 'fill in' time. A walk down Oxford Street on almost any day demonstrates ways in which employees at the bottom of the occupational pile reclaim time. The man whose body is merely an appendage to a metal pole on top of which proclaims the enticements of a half-price sale of sportswear one day, leather goods another. Further down the street on the corner of Tottenham Court Road a plethora of leaflet distributors hand out leaflets, personal stereos in ears, to likely looking candidates for the language schools situated round the corner. Through the use of a personal stereo meaningless time becomes meaningful, yet use is also habitual, mundane and dependent. Adorno's description of time to be filled appears to be consonant with habitual personal-stereo use yet also appears as too deterministic. The 'reflection' that 'might otherwise leap across the workaday world and set it on fire' has already occurred in the experience of many personal-stereo users. The 'fire' is sublimated through the use of a personal stereo.

Lefebvre is at one with Adorno on the inadequacy of a simple parcelling up of experienced time into 'leisure' and 'work'. But Lefebvre posits a 'spontaneity' to the everyday that avoids the total colonization of experience. This resistance is not located in the nature of the 'subject' but in the nature of the phenomenology of 'experience':

> Moreover, the worker craves a sharp break with his work, a compensation. He looks for this in leisure seen as entertainment or distraction. In this way leisure appears as the non everyday in the everyday. We cannot step beyond the everyday. The marvellous can only continue to exist in fiction and the illusions that people share. There is no escape. And yet we wish to have the illusion of escape as near to hand as possible. An illusion not entirely illusory, but constituting a 'world' both apparent and real (the reality of appearances and the apparently real) quite different from the everyday world yet as open ended and as closely dovetailed into the everyday as possible. (Lefebvre 1991b, p. 40)

For Lefebvre the partly illusory nature or compensatory factor in the above experiences does not detract from the fact that they still might be understood as oppositional. This oppositional stance within exper-iential time is often relegated to aesthetics in Adorno's work. Adorno describes this experience as a form of 'compensatory metaphysics' which he perceives as being attached to the inscription of the mundane everyday through music reception in the following:

> Once men have remedies, however poor, against boredom, they are no longer willing to put up with boredom; this contributes to the mass base of musical consumption. It demonstrates a disproportion between condition and potential, between the boredom to which men are still prone and the possible, if unsuccessful, arrangement of life in which boredom would vanish ... But people dread time, and so they invent compensatory metaphysics of time because they blame time for the fact

that in the reified world they no longer feel really alive. This is what the music talks them out of. It confirms the society it entertains. The colour of the inner sense, the bright, detailed imagery of the flow of time, assures a man that within the monotony of universal comparability there is still something particular. (Adorno 1976a, p. 48)

I rather interpret 'compensatory metaphysics as experientially patterned into the habitual daily experience of subjects. The intensity and power of users' description of listening point to both the effectiveness and qualitative transformation of experience through listening. The 'colouring of the inner sense' is achieved in public in a manner unachievable by any other means. Use provides an effective cultural remedy to the onset of perceived 'empty' time:

I've always got the Walkman on. I can't stand sitting on the bus. I get bored. (Claire: interview number 48)

I hate being on a train or bus without having it if I'm by myself. I get really bored. I just like to have something to listen to. (Catriona: interview number 14)

The expectation of having time filled in becomes a normal state for users:

I'm surrounded by music all the time. I can't go a day without having music for more than ten minutes. I listen as often as possible. I'd listen to music for twenty-four hours a day if I could. (Matt: interview number 19)

These users are not responding to the unfree time of work but rather to a cultural expectation and perception of time to be filled. Time spent alone without sound often represents empty time experienced as boring. Users can resort to forms of compensatory metaphysics in which the subjective appropriation of time is narrativized or transmuted into pleasure time. On an everyday level the user translates the 'potential' into the 'conditional' but for only so long as the personal stereo is used. Boredom is perceived of as a continual threat lying beyond the use of the personal stereo. Adorno's description of music providing the 'colour' to the 'inner sense', the 'particular' within the 'ever the same' correlates strongly with personal stereo users' descriptions of daily experience. Music heightens experience within industrial culture:

Rather what music colours is the desolation of the inner sense . . . It is the decoration of empty time. (Adorno 1976a, p. 48)

This fear of empty time is commented upon by many users:

It's almost as if the Walkman is part of my anatomy. As soon as it's off I notice the silence. I've actually been in panic situations when the batteries have run down. The silence is really noticeable. It gets you . . . The silence is really freaky for me. It's almost like a void if you like. (Jade: interview number 13)

Time experienced without it being parcelled up by music becomes in Adorno's terms: 'something spatial and narrow at the same time, like an infinitely long, dark hallway' (Adorno 1973). Personal-stereo users are thus understood as constructing an imaginary or compensatory time in order to dis-attend the infinity of mundane time:

Because you're being entertained (listening to the Walkman) or having your senses stimulated in a way I'm enjoying. That means time appears to pass faster. Time to enjoy yourself. You don't really think of time when you're enjoying yourself. (Karin: interview number 18)

The use of personal stereos represents an everyday adjustment to this insight by the use of newer, more effective technological means. Users describe the 'bright, detailed imagery of the flow of time' experienced through personal-stereo use just use as they describe the fear of that 'long dark hallway' of time without it.

Notes

1. Osborne defines the difference between linear time and cyclical time as follows:

The everyday is situated at the intersection of two modes of repetition: the cyclical, which dominates nature, and the linear which dominates the processes known as 'rational' . . . In modern life the repetitive gestures tends to mask and to crush the cycles. The everyday imposes its own monotony. It is the invariable constant of the variation it envelops. The days follow one another and resemble one another, and yet – and here lies the contradiction at the heart of everydayness – everything changes. But the change is programmed: obsolescence is planned. Production anticipates reproduction; production produces change in such a way as to superimpose the impression of speed on that of monotony. (Osborne 1995, p. 196)

2. 'Compensatory metaphysics' is a term used by Adorno to refer to a person's rebellion against time, often experienced through the consumption of products of the culture industry.

Part II

An Ethnography of Auditory Looking, Aesthetics and Interpersonal Urban Relations

Empowering the 'Gaze': Personal Stereos and the Hidden Look

The interpersonal relationships of people in big cities are characterised by a markedly greater emphasis on the use of the eyes than of the ears. This can be attributed to the institution of public conveyances. Before buses, railroads and trains became fully established during the nineteenth century, people were never in a position to have to stare at one another for minutes or even hours on end without exchanging words . . . [Urban conditions require] an inner barrier between people, a barrier, however, that is indispensable for the modern form of life. For the jostling crowdedness and the motley disorder of metropolitan communication would simply be unbearable without psychological distance. Since contemporary urban culture, with its commercial, professional and social intercourse, forces us to be physically close to an enormous number of people, sensitive and nervous people would sink into despair if the objectification of social relationships did not bring with it an inner boundary and reserve.

Simmel, *The Metropolis and Mental Life*

People stood on local platforms staring nowhere. A look they'd been practising for years. Speeding past, he wondered who they really were.

D. DeLillo, *Libra*

In ordinary railway and bus seating in America, passengers who feel overcrowded may be able to send their eyes out the window, thereby vicariously extending their personal space.

E. Goffman, *Relations in Public*

Not knowing where to put one's eyes whilst travelling through the spaces of the city is a dominant concern amongst urban theorists. The above quotes reflect strategies that subjects use to avoid the perceived social discomfort and embarrassment of the urban 'look'. How do personal-stereo users manage the 'look'? We know that users often establish a zone of separateness within urban spaces in order to create a measure of control over that environment. Yet how does this fit in with the standard accounts of urban looking expressed above? Simmel in the first quote describes Berlin at the beginning of this century where the immense changes in urban geography of the period resulted in the forcible mixing of different sections and classes of people in the city. The fragile strategies whereby subjects attempt to maintain those bourgeois rituals of civility and etiquette are highlighted in his analysis. These strategies are the 'mute stare' coupled with a sense of vulnerability and unease as to where the eyes should rest. This results, in Simmel's analysis, in a retreat into a self-enclosed mode, referred to as an 'inner barrier', that creates a sense of 'reserve' in the urban traveller that becomes 'second nature' to them.

Goffman's subject, in contrast to this, stares out into space through the windows of a railway carriage in order to create a space. Possessed space thus becomes the horizon of the subjects' vision. Other people lose their materiality because they are not seen or attended to. If the subjects' thoughts are placed literally in front of them, then the sense of subjective space is increased to the visual horizon of the subject. This constitutes, for Goffman, a successful method of avoiding the stare and any resultant sense of discomfort.

DeLillo's New Yorkers stand on tube platforms looking distractedly out into an amorphous space. They are careful to avoid the direct glance of the 'other' using this as a strategy of urban survival. The spaces of the city, at least the underground, are described as places of incipient danger and in order to ensure survival one mustn't engage the 'look' of the 'other' for fear of intruding, much the same as drinkers in some public houses will sit and stare at their drinks for fear of offending anyone with a 'look'. These observations; Simmel's, Goffman's and DeLillo's all have a certain exteriority attached to them. Subjects are perceived to be responding to the immutability of their surroundings. Common to all is the defending of some assumed notion of private space. Their responses are all externalist; the woman looks vacantly out of the window; subjects practice their non-looks on station platforms and so on. Common to these observations is an absent interiority. My account of auditory looking and the nature of a technologized auditory construction of urban space is rather undertaken through an analysis of users' accounts. In doing so I provide a micro-study of urban 'looking' devoted to an exposition of the distinctive features of auditory looking, addressing what it means to 'look', 'see' or to be 'seen' in public via the use of technology. I refer to personal stereo looking as a form of 'auditory gazing' constituted through personalized sound. It differs fundamentally from the 'look' constituted through the randomized sounds of the street.

Managing the Gaze

The use of a personal stereo permits the user to control the 'gaze' through a variety of interpersonal strategies. The specificity of auditory looking comes across clearly in the following account:

> When you start commuting it's very unsettling not to know where to put your eyes. The Walkman makes you one step removed from the situation. Also the music is quite comforting, or is something familiar superimposed on everything else . . . It's a way of passively acknowledging that they're not going to talk to anyone, and that what's around them is not relevant to them. It blocks out and it certainly alters reality. You're not full there . . . It emphasises the step of removal from where you are. I was thinking about it today watching someone's conversation. I couldn't hear what they were saying at all. So it wasn't like being within five feet of two people having a conversation. (Chris: interview number 11)

Users consistently claim to be 'somewhere else' whilst using personal stereos. Their physical embodiment appears to be of secondary import-ance whilst their management of their mental state appears to be of primary importance. Significantly the circumstances surrounding these states often differ from those examples given above by Simmel and the others, as these mental states are being driven by the facility of the personal stereo and are not necessarily merely a response to the urban environment. The personal stereo replaces the sounds of the outside world with the sounds chosen by the user. Thus, whatever the exper-iential process is, it is inevitably attended to and mediated by the sound coming through the machine. The sound is immediate and often loud and works to rearrange the senses producing an experience of being 'one step removed' from the physical world. Yet, when users do respond to urban overload, in a manner similar to Simmel's description, the use of a personal stereo removes this unsettled feeling by replacing it with itself, thereby acting to distance any feelings of unsettledness. Personal-stereo use acts to transform users' horizons of experience by superimposing itself onto that environment, cloaking the alien with the familiar and in doing so transforms the subjective response to it. The respondent quoted above describes this process as a passive response to the social situation tinged with an element of guilt, 'as if' what was around him should in some sense be relevant to him. This attitude to the social is not typical of users and in this instance resulted in the person using their personal stereo less and less. More typical is the following quote from a woman in her mid twenties:

> It's easier to have eye contact with people, because you can look but you're listening to something else. You don't feel you're intruding in on people, because you're in your own little world. (Stephanie: interview number 42)

The above user both looks and does not look. Eye contact has a different meaning if the recipient of the gaze can see that the person is 'somewhere else', signifying that the gaze is not a penetrative gaze but rather an unintentional or distracted gaze. This type of gaze, according to this user, does not constitute an 'incursion' into the private space of another due to the lack of intentionality held in the gaze. In a sense the look isn't a look at all. The subject is somewhere else in 'her own little world'. The term 'one's own little world' is used repeatedly by respondents to describe their personal stereo states both in public and in private. This particular respondent goes on to make the following observation:

> I'm not always aware of who else has a Walkman on. I wonder where they are because whoever's wearing one is somewhere else. (Stephanie: interview number 42)

Users are often indifferent to the presence of others as this rather common response indicates:

> I often think they are thinking about nothing. They're just going. And I don't see them because I'm so used to it and I've got my Walkman. So I don't see them. (Sirah: interview number 15)

This negation of the external environment can be a totalizing experience and is often encapsulated by an attendant burdensome awareness of the 'eversame' of the everyday urban. The 'other' is often perceived in terms of a blank object, exteriorized automatons on their way to work devoid of thoughts, invisible and of no concern to this user at least. There also appears to to be a staving off of the awareness that she too might be like them if not for the use of her personal stereo that secures her in her own subjectivity. The user is a twenty-year-old woman who is performing her daily journey across London on public transport. The use of her personal stereo relieves the boredom of the journey, but for this user there is also the fear of the anonymity of the the urban, of losing oneself within it, coupled with a fear of the unknown. The city for her has a kind of anonymous danger attached to it:

> I think it's good to keep yourself apart from other people. I feel vulnerable with people I don't know. (Sirah: interview number 15)

She uses technology as a kind of security fix. Along with her personal stereo she now has a mobile phone which she also claims not to be able to be without. The arsenal of mobile technology becomes her 'lifeline' whilst traversing those empty but potentially fearful public spaces (Bauman 1991). Another user describes the world beyond the personal stereo in the following terms:

> When you've got your Walkman on it's like a wall. Decoration. Surround-ings. It's not anyone. (Ed: interview number 59)

The metaphor of a 'wall' aptly describes the impenetrability of the user's state, or desired state, in relation to the geographical space of experience. The world becomes the backcloth to one's own thoughts; people become adjuncts to this, or alternatively are not noticed at all. The following user is not motivated by apprehension as our other user appeared to be, but merely by the superfluity of it all:

> I look around. Look out the window. I guess because from Finchley to High Barnet you're above ground. But you won't really be seeing it. You're just staring blankly at it. You watch the people in the carriage and wonder what they're about but you don't think too hard about it because you've got something else in your head. (Mags: interview number 31)

The dreamlike state of use and the consequent non-look of the user is brought out clearly by the following quote:

Some people might think you're staring at them but I don't. You just look straight ahead, sometimes you don't look around. Then you come to consciousness and realize you've been staring at them for half an hour – and you've not really been looking at them. When you've got your Walkman on your brain tends to – you're listening to the music – nothing else – but when you've got nothing else. You look around. You're just conscious. (Jana: interview number 47)

The look here is a totally unrecognized one; it merely appears. The object of the gaze may not know it, but it isn't a look at all. This user is surprised when she realizes that he has been staring at another person. The awareness comes with the breaking into real time as distinct from personal stereo time. During personal stereo time the subject does not look. Looking is reserved for states when the world floods in. The first respondent whilst thinking vacantly about other passengers also does not really look and is equally 'somewhere else'. The gaze on occasion might also be more aggressive in the sense of being bolstered by the person's own soundtrack and the resulting sense of security derived from this, as is the case in these two young males where use works to empower the gaze:

I feel a bit more confident. So I can just stare at them. (Dan: interview number 22)

Yeh. I stare at people. I won't be staring at them. I'll just be looking at them. (Michael: interview number 40)

Users are sometimes aware of the difference between a personal stereo 'look' and other forms of looking:

[On the bus] I look up, usually I'm looking behind or up at the person if the person opposite is interesting. But I don't look at him or her as a person and I don't even think I'm looking at them. I just, kind of stare straight through them. But I get a lot of people looking straight back. There's different ways of looking at somebody. (Gemma: interview number 24)

Using a personal stereo also permits users to negotiate potentially embarrassing looks from others. The following user expresses feelings of discomfort at being 'stared at' in the close proximity of the tube. A feeling more frequently mentioned by female users:

I'm completely lost on the tube. Completely absorbed. It's just another distraction. I feel quite uncomfortable with that sort of eye contact. It's just so raw on the tube. In the tube I'm just completely out of it. No. I look down really. Sometimes I might have my eyes closed. (Jo: interview number 30)

Whilst the above respondent, a woman in her late twenties, is equally absorbed or 'lost' on the tube this appears to be more of a reaction to embarrassment and as a method of fending off unwanted or incursive looks. Listening to her personal stereo does not make her feel braver on the tube although elsewhere, on the street it does make her feel more assertive. On the tube it merely occupies her time. She avoids glances, looks down and closes her eyes. This differs from the quote below where for this female user the auditory look becomes an omnipotent one with reciprocal gazing perceived as being impossible:

It's like looking through a one-way mirror. I'm looking at them but they can't see me. (Julie: interview number 12)

It is a recurring theme amongst users to refer to looking without being seen. The above description of vision as a one-way mirror is merely the most succinct metaphor for escaping the 'reciprocal gaze'. In this account the viewing subject disappears into an unobserved gaze. In essence a voyeur's gaze of omnipotent control. The role of the personal stereo in this is to make the person's gaze invisible. At the same time her private space remains inviolable whilst she wears her personal stereo, permitting her to perceive the situation as being under control. This can be referred to conceptually as a form of non-reciprocal gazing that embodies an extreme form of asymmetry. This avoidance of the reciprocal gaze means that the subject cannot be fixed. Only as exteriority can she be grasped. This response is mirrored in the following response of a thirty-year-old woman:

I feel more invisible if anything. Just detached. An observer. Invisible in the sense of a detached observer. I feel very, very detached. I can't say I'm detached from other people looking at me. I'm just detached from the normal rigmarole of sirens and screeching breaks . . . I feel more detached from it all, then I feel I can look at them more. Just look at them. See them. I just perceive it differently. I see it. I feel I see it for what it truly is. You see deeper . . . I can really study them and they can't see me. (Jay: interview number 33)

Two processes are operative here; the blocking out of sounds and the auditory look. By blocking out, Jay claims to be able to see more clearly, as if the sounds in her head were constructing a true image or facilitating a true understanding of the subjects of her gaze. It would appear in this instance that the narcissistic gaze is a complement to an empowered gaze. The personal stereo in these cases facilitates a voyeuristic gaze which might be seen to empower the gazer merely because they have worked out a strategy to look and not be seen. In doing so they protect their space and identity from the reciprocal stare. The above example, along with others, demonstrates that the 'voyeuristic' gaze cannot merely be understood in terms of gender categories. Both male and female users feel a sense of empowerment through the use of personal stereos. This does not mean, however, that the social dynamic is the same for both sexes. More women users refer to resorting to personal-stereo use in order to avoid the stare of others.

Avoiding the Gaze: Personal Stereo Use and Social Invisibility

How then do users absent themselves from the gaze of others? Intrinsic to these processes is the reconceptualization of subjective placement in the urban domain. The use of personal stereos replaces the sounds of the outside world with an alternative soundscape which is more immediate and subject to greater control. This replacement function of the personal stereo can be controlled in the sense that the user can adjust the sound levels to suit their circumstances, desire or mood. A consensus is demonstrated in user accounts concerning the transformative nature of use on the subjects' experiences of journeying and their relationship to the outside world. Users typically describe the sound as overwhelmingly enveloping them:

> You become more aware of you and less aware of what's going on. The music is not like a background. It's all around you. It takes over your senses. It can be quite isolating. Walking around I don't feel part of anything. I tend to drift off into nothingness. I'm not thinking about anything or looking at anything. I'm just there physically. I just disappear. (Mags: interview number 31)

> It's just me in my own world. After doing that journey you just ignore people and you're just going. You don't even look. It makes you feel

almost, like more powerful. I feel much more comfortable with a Walkman on, standing at the bus stop than with nothing at all. (Paul: interview number 9)

It's very insular you know. It's just very much me. You know. On my own sort of stuff and obviously I snap out of it once I get to my destination. (Betty: interview number 34)

It enables me to sort of bring my own dreamworld. Because I have familiar sounds with my music that I know and sort of cut out people around me. So the music is familiar. There's nothing new happening. I can go into my own perfect dreamworld where everything is as I want it. (Magnus: interview number 21)

Users appear to achieve, at least subjectively, a sense of public invisibility. They essentially 'disappear' as interacting subjects withdrawing into various states of the purely subjective. Subjective in the sense of focusing or attending to themselves. This attention can be non-intentional and is described by some users passively as taking over their senses. The immediacy of the personal stereo experience overrides the functioning of the other senses which become subordinate to the vivid mental and physical experience of listening to music. Sometimes this appears to be intentional whilst at other times it is merely the response to the music understood as a form of distracted drifting. Users frequently report that they drift in and drift out of their journeys. The power to drift in and out at will is again seen as a pleasurable form of control.

The relationship between public and private space also appears to be transformed in the above accounts as users negate any meanings that the public might have or might accurately be seen as having. Public spaces are voided of meaning and are represented as 'dead' spaces to be traversed as easily and as pleasurably as possible. Alternatively, environments such as trains or buses which merely transport the user through urban space to somewhere they either want to go or have to go are put to one side. Public space in this instance is not merely transformed into a private sphere but rather negated so as to prioritize the private. As such, personal stereos facilitate a host of new options for dealing with both the public in its immediacy together with helping the user deal with their own private experiences, desires and moods. This activity isn't fully grasped by merely transposing categories of active or passive onto the behaviour. In the following example the use of a personal stereo becomes a self conscious barrier, a shield against the social, against both the 'look' as well as a shield to hide feelings of insecurity:

> I'm a shy person at times. My Walkman hides me away from that. (Jade: interview number 13)

The use of a personal stereo can also function to enhance any situation by turning a potential anxiety into a pleasurable and personal experience. Personal, inasmuch as the following user maintains that other people in the street merely have the same experience, whilst she possesses something unique which is 'hers'. The user, in effect, transcends her empirically viewed self:

> I'm aware of the fact that I'm different from other people walking down the street because I'm not listening to the sounds they can hear. I'm listening to my music. But it doesn't make me feel anxious. It puts me in a good mood actually. You don't feel lonely. It's your own environment. It's like you're making something pleasurable you can do by yourself and enjoy it. (Sara: interview number 50)

The above example is also an alternative way of claiming private space. Personal space, as we have seen, is often represented in terms of the users thoughts, mood or volition and can be understood either as an active focusing on the experience of being elevated beyond the spatial present or in the giving oneself up to it:

> I might be concentrating on the music but my mind might be somewhere else as well . . . It depends what you're listening to. You might start marching to the music or the other extreme. Being in a total dream. Not being aware of anything. I kind of feel it's more unreal in a way. It's a kind of escapism. It's time out. (Gemma: interview number 24)

Users frequently describing experience in terms of two 'worlds'; the world in the head of the user with its own rearrangement of the senses and the world in which this takes place and which has a different arrangement and often a different sense of time and movement attached to it:

> It just separates you really. Because there's just you and the music and there's just nothing else that you need to talk about with anyone. If you want to think you can. (Donna: interview number 52)

Escape is also a frequent metaphor used by users. The following respondent, a 27-year-old woman lists what she might successfully be escaping from whilst using her personal stereo:

> Your nightmare journey. Listening to people arguing or yapping on the bus. Time out before the reality of where you're going. It depends on the end of the journey. You might be pretending that really you're not going to where you're going and the situation you're going into. So it's time out in a nice way. Or alternatively it could be psyching yourself up for whoever you're seeing. (Louise: interview number 16)

Personal stereos can be used to cope with, to avoid or to transform both public experience and/or the subjective, intentional narrative of the user. Transforming the perceived unpleasantness of the journey and the interruptive nature of time spent in public is an important method of coping with or enhancing one's own personal intentions or projects. These strategies of management are not necessarily derived, as the above accounts demonstrate, as a response to the physical environment moved through, in contrast to those accounts stemming from the work of Simmel.

Clearing a Space for Looking

Paradoxically some users claim that they see more clearly through the use of a personal stereo. In the light of the analysis above of the ways in which personal stereos are used to create non-reciprocal gazing, this claim needs to be investigated. The following examples are typical:

> I like to see. I like to see exactly and I feel I'm absorbing more because the music is helping me concentrate and because it's so familiar to me I don't have to listen to it so attentively. I know what's coming and I can almost look for that. (Ron: interview number 58)

> I'm locking myself in a bit more. It locks the rest of the world out, but then, maybe it doesn't. I think the music also helps me to relate to the outside world. I'll start to notice things more because of the music sometimes. There's nothing to distract you. There's just the journey and the music. (Robina: interview number 35)

Personal stereo's appear to function as a clarifier in the above examples. The perceived auditory chaos of the urban environment is overlain by the managed industrialized sounds of the personal stereo which are 'known'. It is this sense of the familiar that enables the users to clarify their looking. In the following example the 'look' accompanies the user's own movement and sound:

> I do feel engaged because I'm seeing it. If I look at a mountain I can see its peak, you know. I can see it. If I'm listening to something beautiful in the background it can only add to it. (Jay: interview number 33)

This look is an aestheticized look in which the narcissistic orientation of the looker predominates. The engagement with the visual becomes real with the added 'beautiful background' to heighten the visual component of experience. In doing so the experience becomes phantasmagoric (Benjamin), a spectacle (Debord). The following user describes lingering on a train platform entranced by the scene, too entranced to catch his train:

> In a way when you're walking it does make you engage with your surroundings more that I otherwise would. I wouldn't normally stop and watch people walking up and down the stairs. Whereas I would do that, or miss a train just so I could hear this tune in this space. (Chris: interview number 11)

Cyclists increasingly wear personal stereos as they traverse the city. Life expectancy demands that they remain visually attentive. Users describe the chaotic sounds of the road as being recessed and replaced by the clarity and predicability of personal stereo sounds. For cyclists, who cannot hear the sounds of the street, it is necessary to have to 'look' more clearly. This is translated into more effective viewing in the sense of clearing space in the mind for the uninterrupted concentration of the cyclist. The fact that nothing can be heard behind the cyclist is conveniently ignored by the following user:

> I'm visually more aware [on the bike]. Because you're aware that you're not listening. I'm more focused. More visually defined. I never lose myself in the music completely. (Stephanie: interview number 42)

Ironically, some cyclists claim that they would be too frightened to cycle around London without using a personal stereo. This despite the awareness that reaction time to the unexpected is often slower with its use. In effect hearing has to be replaced by sight.

I think I become more aware when I've got my Walkman because you have to. I'm not stupid enough to walk in the middle of the road with it. But you become more aware because normally when you cross the road you can hear the sound of the cars. You have to be more aware. So I feel you're more connected with things around you in a way. I'm a very aware person. So I'm always looking around. (Ben: interview number 41)

The complexity and potentially contradictory nature of auditory looking is brought out in the following quote:

I suppose it makes everything surreal, like a dreamlike state because without the sound to go with your vision . . . disorientates everything and there's a different sound to the visual side . . . the world around. Well. It just doesn't fit in with it . . . It's strange. I suppose more distant because I can't hear. I suppose I am more distant. But I'm more aware visually. I'm quite a visual person. (Karin: interview number 18)

This perceptive comment points to an awareness of a parallel sense of being in the world and the disorientation that stems from an awareness of this coupling. The expectation that certain movements will be attended by specific sounds that are being replaced by one's own sounds creates a feeling or visual image in this user that she associates with surrealism by which she means the juxtaposing of two dissimilar things placed into a naturalistic setting. However, respondents, in discussing visual clarity, appear to refer to an awareness of a generalized 'outside' rather than to the process of interactive gazing. When an auditory look is focused it often appears to be an aestheticized one. Alternatively, the auditory gaze functions as an urban strategy whereby users attempt to manage the nature of the urban 'look' so as to control it.

s e v e n

Filmic Cities and Aesthetic Experience

I think all concepts of the 'postmodern' have at least one affirmative feature in common, viz. To see in the process of the 'dissolution of the social' the chance for an expansion of aesthetic freedom for individuals.

A. Honneth, *Pluralization and Recognition*

Film creates a dreaming space which all of us occupy.

D. DiLillo, *Libra*

The massive outer world has lost its weight, it has been freed from space, time and causality, and has been clothed in forms of our own consciousness.

H. Mustenberg, *The Film: A Psychological Study*

The aestheticization of the urban is well documented in the literature on urban habitation. Indeed it is one of the central motifs of much work that concentrates on the visual nature of aesthetic appropriation. Richard Sennett's (1990, 1994) work illuminates the visual prioritization of much urban experience which he contrasts to the decline of speech and touch in urban culture. Bauman (1993) also discusses the aesthetics of urban looking, whilst others focus upon this mode of experience through a re-appropriation of Benjamin's account of 'flânerie' (Tester 1994). From this point of view, personal-stereo users become technologized *flâneurs*. In this chapter I interrogate the meaning and variety of 'aesthetic looking' through personal-stereo user accounts and in doing so I produce a systematic analysis of urban aesthetic looking that contests existing accounts.

85

Aesthetic experience is of course one form of 'relational' experience, and in urban studies it is invariably understood in terms of a visual experience that either possesses no significant relational qualities or relatively harmless ones:

> The beauty of 'aesthetic control' – the unclouded beauty, beauty unspoiled by the fear of danger, guilty conscience or apprehension of shame – is its inconsequentiality. This control will not intrude into the realities of the controlled. It will not limit their options. It puts the spectator into the director's chair – with the actors unaware of who is sitting there, of the chair itself, even of being potential objects of the directors attention. Aesthetic control, unlike any other, gruesome or sinister social control which it playfully emulates, allows to thrive the contingency of life which social spacing strove to confine or stifle. Inconsequentiality of aesthetic control is what makes it's pleasures unclouded . . . I make them [people] into whatever I wish. I am in charge; I invest their encounter with meaning. (Bauman 1993, p. 6)

The asymmetrical nature of the aesthetic mode of social recreation is appropriately captured in this description, yet the ramifications of this form of social asymmetry when broadened out into a mode of 'being in the world' is not fully articulated. Honneth in contrast to this perceives the aesthetic as inversely proportional to the realization of a habitable social (Honneth 1992).

What role does aesthetic experience play in the daily use of personal stereos? The use of personal stereos greatly expands the possibilities for users to aesthetically recreate their daily experience. Existing accounts of the use of personal stereos are often framed around notions of an aesthetically consuming public (Chambers 1994; Hosokawa 1984). However these accounts are firmly rooted in visual epistemologies of experience, and discount the specifically auditory nature of experience in general and looking in particular. In the previous chapter I articulated the specificity of 'auditory looking' coupled with an understanding of personal-stereo use that is motivated as much by private concerns as users' responses to the physical urban environment. In analysing auditory forms of the aesthetic I question existing accounts of the everyday significance of such behaviour.

Personal-stereo users often refer to their experiences as being 'cinematic' in nature. In the following pages I enquire into the possible meanings attached to such descriptions. Users describe filmic experience in a variety of ways. An initial distinction can be made between specific recreations of filmic-type experience with personal narratives attached to them and more generalized descriptions of the world appearing to be like a film (which is sometimes encountered in users responses). Generalized accounts take the following forms:

I find it quite weird watching things that you normally associate certain sounds with, like the sounds of walking up and down the stairs or tubes coming in and out. All those things you hear. Like when you've got your Walkman on you don't hear any of those. You've got your own soundtrack to them as it were. (Karin: interview number 18)

I like to watch people with the music. You see all the people. Everybody's doing something. But you see them in the light of the music and they can't hear that music. When I listen to my tape I have the feeling that everybody else is far away. I like to watch, not necessarily people, also places. Everything . . . It's nice with my Walkman. I see all the people, like from far away. Everybody's busy with something. You don't know what. Everybody's got a story and you try to read it. I see the lights. Everything. Without the Walkman, all their voices and noises would disturb me and maybe I would hate the people. With the Walkman I just see them. I don't actually hear them. So I idolize them. Maybe think of them much better things than they actually do and are. It makes me see people in a different way. (Claudia: interview number 38)

The experience of using personal stereos is often described as all engulfing with users describing being saturated with sound. The sensations and experiences in their heads are normally described as more direct or heightened that anything beyond them. The above quotes point to a disjunction between the experiencing subject and the world of movement and sounds beyond as well as a recreation of general narrative to music without any specific script. The first quote refers more to the disjunction between conceptual and physical space whilst the second is more aesthetic in its recreation of meaning constructed through the use of a personal stereo. However, to investigate the variety of meanings attached to descriptions of 'cinematic' experience it is necessary to analyse specific examples in greater depth. In order to do this I provide five recreated narrative examples. Each account is recreated in the spirit of the text with no content material added but merely a situating narrative reconstructed directly from the interview material.

Five Personal Stereo Stories

Story Number One: (Mags: interview number 31)

It's two o'clock in the morning. It's raining heavily in the street. Mag's looks out of her window and decides she would like to walk; she likes the rain at night. The street is deserted. She hears the sound of the rain on the pavement. She takes a tape from a pile scattered randomly on the floor. Puts her coat on, picks up her personal stereo and walks out the door. As she closes the door, she turns the volume up using the switch on her headphone lead. She keeps her finger on the volume control and starts walking ready to change the volume if she sees anybody approach. She's relieved; the music on the tape is U2; she knows it well. She turns the volume up till the music seems to wash through her, and walks:

> It heightens. Everything becomes filmic. When you see things and when you have music on you hear a sound. I know that when you put music to an actual image it becomes part of it. Actually what I do is go out for a walk when it's pouring with rain with a Walkman on.

She can no longer hear the sound of the rain, but she feels it and can see it. The music transforms the scene in the following way:

> It makes it filmic. It seems more like a scene and you can imagine yourself as the tortured heroine from this film walking along in the rain and all this score . . . music blasting! You're the heroine. You can see yourself as if on the screen. You see what's in front of you.

The music on her personal stereo isn't film music. It's just a tape that she knows well. She uses the music to construct her own scenario with herself in it:

> You hear it and you try to apply it to your surroundings. A tape you've listened to a lot. That you know really well. Lyrics that you've heard lots of times but you might decide that night to apply some importance to them when you play the scenario.

So she walks down the empty street, the tortured heroine to her own movie. Is she the heroine or is she mimicking someone else being the heroine?

> Both I suppose. I don't have a film in my head that I relate to.

The image is not specific, it doesn't necessarily remind her of a scene but is rather her own creation taken from a stock of memories of heroines from films half forgotten, scenes barely remembered or scenes from the multitude of pop videos watched distractedly, or maybe even a trace from childhood novels of romance read from under the bedclothes deep into the night (extrapolation from the text of the interview).

Story Number Two: (Dorinda: interview number 32)

Dorinda rushes out of the flat. She's late again. It's a bright summers morning. She switches on her personal stereo, clips it to her belt and gets on her bike. The streets are busy and she decides to take her normal detour through the park. The music swells up. It's her favourite personal stereo tape. Violins, Spanish guitar:

> I listen to *1492* a lot which is the Conquest. Christopher Columbus, which says it all really. Its very much about journeys and it builds. It gives your journey more significance.

As she cycles her body appears to lose it's weight, the bike appears to be moving on its own to the music, but with her guiding it:

> It's just amazing. It has its prime moments, has its tranquil moments.

She's cycling quite fast, she just has the sound of the sweeping violins in her ears, she faintly hears the siren of a police car or ambulance. She turns into St James's Park and cycles on the footpath. Everything seems more vivid to her:

> On the bike you're very visually dependent. You're so visually dependent and here you are being provided with music to go with it and it's music you've chosen, and it can alter your perspective on things . . . It's a park, it's nicer than going on the road when you've got music to go with it, it will highlight certain things that you see, or it can do. I think it lends significance to what you're seeing, depending on what you're listening to.

She picks her music carefully. It has to fit, to be in tune with her mood and her surroundings. She constructs imaginary scenarios to what she sees whilst she cycles. She cycles past two people walking in the park.

She imagines them as lovers, making up after a quarrel. She cycles along constructing her own script. When she does this, she is focusing on outside, she doesn't think so much about herself, her own problems.

> Without the Walkman, you wouldn't, you might not even wonder. It's no significance. Suddenly you're listening to *1492* and it's like 'Are they lovers?' You get caught up. You look at things differently, the pond, the flowers become more flowery. Things are enhanced, moments are enhanced . . . When there's music I think less. It becomes more my journey. It becomes more emotional. It becomes more of a sensory experience and it's lovely.

Yet whilst she's constructing her scenario in tune to the music she doesn't see it as her own creation, her own direction:

> It's weird isn't it. It's happening around me. No. I'm a viewer. I'm a viewer and I'm assimilating what I see. So it's more like watching a film, but it's my life.

Dorinda constructs a fleeting narrative out of her journey. This imaginary narrative she reflectively sees as a form of control:

> But the fact that I'm seeing two people and imagining they're lovers. It's not about them. It's about me. It's my relationship to them. It brings it back to me. It's very self-indulgent to be riding a bike with a Walkman. Total control.

The control only works if the music is right though. Cycling in the evening and not wishing to play fast, moving music Robina says:

> It just doesn't suit the films, the night-time film soundtrack that's my life. Not the soundtrack. You know what I mean.

Story Number Three: (Catriona: interview number 14)

Catriona wears her personal stereo a lot, she often daydreams with it on. She likes going to movies. Just recently she has gotten very interested in the Quentin Tarantino movies *Reservoir Dogs* and *Pulp Fiction*. She has gone out and bought both soundtracks and she plays them repeatedly on her personal stereo. The music from these films makes her feel happy, confident. She likes the music to be loud. The fact that it is film music means that it has a different significance for her than if it was her normal listening music:

> Because you can remember the scene. Two of the songs from *Reservoir Dogs*. I can remember exactly the scenes so I think about that. It's funny because the opening scene, this first song, this soundtrack. They're all walking down the street. They've all got their suits on. I was listening to it the other day when I was walking down the street and the first track came on. I didn't feel I was in the film but I could remember the feeling of the film listening to that song.

The feeling of the film remembered makes her feel more confident She plays the soundtrack loud so that nothing else intrudes on her listening:

> A friend of mine had just dropped me at Paddington. I had to walk to the tube stop. I put on *Reservoir Dogs*. This song at the beginning of the soundtrack. I just felt like I was really strutting. I'm sure I wasn't but that's what it felt like. I was walking in time to the music.

The mood of the film is recreated through the music and becomes a part of Cartiona's persona for that part of her journey.

Story Number Four: (Magnus: interview number 21)

Magnus likes to enhance his environment and fantasizes to music on his personal stereo. He describes his actual environment as boring. He chooses his music and creates an adventure out of his normal but mundane journey. He describes the wearing of his personal stereo in town as creating a filmic situation in which he is a the central player:

> It's sort of like making my life a film. Like you have the sound, the soundtrack in the back.

Magnus has a certain idea of the type of film he likes to be in. His hometown has an old square in it. He creates the image of:

> Something big with a lot of people, a lot of costumes, or sometimes like a Merchant Ivory film. There is this central square and then at the end there are stairs leading to the town. There is an old fortification. When I walk down to the centre of town I have to walk down these stairs and

you walk down these stairs with some Beethoven or something. It makes it more interesting. Walking down you feel like coming down in a film.

So Magnus is placing himself in a period film, the music isn't film music but merely creates the mood to enhance the surroundings as if it were film music. More specifically he then begins to imagine or to create specific scenarios to go with the general scene transforming the mundane into an adventure where he uses his imagination to place himself in the centre of a transformed scenario, heightening its significance and creating a world of expectation:

I like to daydream. Imagine things. What might happen if I go round that corner. What might happen there. What if that person were standing there.

Magnus sees this as a form of perfect control to use his term:

It enables me to sort of bring my own dreamworld. Because I have the familiar sounds with my music that I know and sort of cut out people. So the music is familiar. I can go into my perfect dreamworld where everything is as I want it.

Magnus's journeying with his personal stereo becomes an attempt to construct an imaginary world, a perfect image of his own fantasy:

Everything is exactly as I want it. Everybody is nice, everybody is happy, everyone is beautiful. The sun is always shining. I can do whatever I like basically.

Story Number Five: (Jade: interview number 13)

The following comes from extracts of the diary Jade kept describing the use of his personal stereo:

Get on the bus going home. I'm listening to Rap music. Thinking about the films I've watched. Trying to find things in *Goodfellas* that I've seen in other films. The journey is so long because of the traffic. I get so tense that I end up becoming a character from *Goodfellas* for fifteen minutes. I reach Our Price. Turn off my Walkman and it's fine to get in character.

I hear a sample from a movie on the song I'm listening to. It's from *A Few Dollars More*. Now I think about the scenes from that film. I then find that my mood has changed at work because whenever I speak to the colleague from Hell, I'm very cold and become a verbal bounty hunter. Whenever he says something I just shoot him with short cool blasts of verbal abuse and collect the reward which is a barrel of laughs.

Catch the bus. I'm listening to the soundtrack of *Pulp Fiction* which puts me in a better mood. While I'm listening to it I envisage myself in the film. That's how absorbed the film's got me. Sometimes I wish I was the bad guy in life with all those witty lines that just shuts people up. So I mentally picture myself in Pulp Fiction except that there would be a few more murders and that Ingrid Bergman, Liz Taylor, Deborah Kerr were in it. Then I arrive at work in character repeating all the lines from ages past.

The image is visualized and also represents the fantasized recreation of a role controlled by the person. The mimetic function of music and film is especially apparent in the above example from a respondent's diary where the language also takes on the narrative and tone of the films mentioned.

The above examples demonstrate a variety of meanings given to filmic experience that varies according to the subject and situation. In the first example Mags attempts to recreate the physicality or atmosphere of a film by physically going out in the dark. She is in the centre of her movie yet her surroundings are perceived to be real; for example it has to be raining. She doesn't appear able or willing to transform a scene into one where it is raining. This would fit in with her belief that using her personal stereo during the day is not so filmic for her. Her normal day-to-day use does not conjure up these images for her. There is a similarity in Mag's description of filmic experience with the actual experience of being in the cinema. She is in a darkened space where she looks ahead of herself in isolation and she places herself in the position of being central, and literally she is the heroine in the centre of the movie. She has no plot, just the sensation of being the heroine on a windswept night: 'you see yourself as if on a screen'. The physical environment also has to be deserted for the experience to fulfil it's potential.

The second example of Dorinda constructing her scenario on her bicycle is very different. She constructs the experience as one of projection. She looks out and constructs the narrative as if directing it. For her, the environment and the characters in it provide a fragmented, fleeting mode of appropriation. She is, of course, moving faster on her bike. People assume the role of characters in her film; the film essentially being her journey: 'the night-time film soundtrack that's my life'. For this she needs film music which is the soundtrack to a film about a journey, like her own in that respect. Ironically she uses *1492*, the journey of Columbus which can also be seen as a journey where the protagonists construct the journey and its purpose out of their own myths with the characters met functioning as fictional creations of their own colonial imaginations. Essentially the example of the two lovers/characters works in much the same way and is a relationship of power as Dorinda reflectively acknowledges. She, unlike Mags, does not necessarily place herself as a character in her narrative but as a viewer. The scene is created as a fictional narrative, not as a part of her autobiography. Although she does mention the soundtrack to the 'film of her life' this appears to be generalized.

Catriona's transformation of her world differs from this. She, like Dorinda uses specific film music, in this case most recently *Reservoir Dogs* and *Pulp Fiction*. She plays the soundtracks repeatedly, liking the music but also recreating the atmosphere of the actual movie in her mind. She recollects the various scenes from the film, visualizes them whilst walking. She doesn't attempt to impose herself onto the scene, merely to recreate it in her head. She also does not try to transform her surroundings. So there is no visual transformation of the meaning of her surroundings. Her filmic experience is totally hermetic to herself and the music. This, however, is translated into her physical movements which represent a greater confidence as she walks in time to the music through the street. Although this appears to be as much a response to the beat of the music as any characterisation of herself in the film. The visual element in Catriona's re-experiencing is lacking. The experience is one of internal recreation. In doing so the traversed world is put into the background. This would fit in with Catriona's descriptions of disorientation with her environment and absentmindedness whilst wearing her personal stereo.

Jade's diary entries, whilst appear similar to Catriona's in as much as no visual heightening or recreation takes place in his filmic recreation of experience, differ in all other respects. Jade transform's his attitude to social interaction through film characterization bringing the character of the lead into play in his actual dealings with others. Whilst listening to film music, more often than not Westerns, but also *film noir* and gangster movies, Jade puts himself into the leading character role and becomes a Clint Eastwood or John Travolta, mimicking their language or their perceived manner in 'dealing' with situations. He becomes the star who sorts things out; who nobody successfully 'messes' with. He has an omnipotent fantasy in his dealings with others, especially in times of tension or conflict. It is interesting that Jade knows the movies well enough to be able to mimic the phrases used by the central characters. The film music puts him into 'character' or 'mood'; there is no indication that Jade finds it easy to do this without listening to music. He listens on his journeys to and from work and so puts himself into character on arrival. Whilst on the bus he recreates the movie as does Catriona but imaginatively recreates the film, filling it with his favourite screen stars, whilst always keeping the central character 'in character'.

Magnus's account on the face of it appears to be similar to Mags's although with a heightened sense of control. His 'dreamworld' might be seen to be structurally similar to hers. However, he seems to literally re-imagine his surroundings, placing them into a scene of a movie thus making it conform to his desires by transforming it into a romantic period piece with music to suit the surroundings. Having the right music is very important in this instance. He, unlike Mags, will populate his scene with others who become the props to his fantasy. Magnus lays great stress of the perfection of his creation. It becomes a function of his need to perceive things in terms of perfect control. His life for this period of time becomes perfect, stating that 'I can do anything that I want.' Perfection represents the absence of contradiction in this perfect aesthetic of subjective control and imagination. He, like Mags, is in the centre of his movie but he actively constructs possible adventures, like imagining what might happen to him if he takes a left turn rather than a right thus creating an adventure out of the normal and mundane.

These five examples have been discussed in detail as they illustrate the varied ways in which the notion of filmic experience manifests itself among personal-stereo users, and draws us into the description of 'filmic' as either being an interior flow of experience, or an aesthetic that imaginatively appropriates or integrates the world into itself. We can see from these examples that filmic experience need not be particularly visual but might concentrate on the mood of a scene or on a mimicking of characters from films. When it is visual the subject might recreate the scene according to some imaginary film or altern-atively the people in the actual surroundings are transformed into characters, as extras to the subjective drama as it unfolds. Sometimes, in order for the illusion to be effective, there must be no people present to intrude into the experience. All these examples are based on the active recreation of some aspect of their journeying and all take place whilst the person is alone.

Almost any experience can be construed as filmic by personal-stereo users. A common thread running through the above experiences is one of attempted control of the environment or mood and the reappropriation or reassertion of the power of the user. Music does not merely function as a definer of the experience in any determinate way, as the above examples demonstrate, but appears to be the necessary spark to a spectrum of aesthetic recreations of their experiences in public. However, there is an ambivalence attached to this form of aesthetic experience as the following user puts it:

> I remember reading a comment that it changes your life. It's like living in a movie. I noticed that today. There's one particular tape that I used to listen to four years ago, a particularly wonderful piece of music. When I was in the Barbican today watching all the people, it was like a German expressionist film . . . I don't think it's a good thing to make your life like a movie. I didn't think about it at the time. It emphasizes the step of removal from where you are. (Chris: interview number 11)

The above analysis of aesthetic looking has demonstrated a spectrum of filmic-type experiences described by users. They are only partially visual. The use of personal stereos, therefore, does not unambiguously support theories that discuss the visual prioritization of urban experience. Indeed use appears in significant ways to contradict notions of visuality. Even within the role of aesthetic recreation the geographically visual is often not primarily attended to but merely used as a backcloth. The aesthetic recreation or reappropriation of the urban through the act of looking is mediated through the subjects' desires which are stimulated both by desire and music. Sometimes the physical scene is endowed with new meaning, a background to their imaginary drama, at other times the drama is redrawn as an interior recollection or mental orientation or mood where the external world isn't really attended to at all. This appears to demonstrate that standard accounts of non-auditory looking cannot be transposed onto forms of auditory looking without loss of meaning. Therefore the notion that personal-stereo users are engaged in acts of urban *flânerie* are thrown into doubt. The significance of an auditory aesthetic will be taken up in Chapter Twelve in which personal-stereo use will be contextualized within the use of a range of other consumer communication technologies.

The Asymmetrical Urban: The Role of Personal Stereos in Managing Interpersonal Behaviour

The language of everyday life is still invested with a knowledge – which we take for granted – that we implicitly owe our integrity to the receipt of approval or recognition from other persons.

A. Honneth, *The Fragmented World of the Social*

My sense of myself, of the footing I am on with others, is in large part also embodied. The deference I owe you is carried in the distance I stand from you, in the way I fall silent when you start to speak, in the way I hold myself in your presence. Alternatively, the sense I have of my own importance is carried in the way I swagger. Indeed, some of the most pervasive features of my attitude to the world and to others is encoded in the way I project myself in public space; whether I am macho, or timid, or eager to please, or calm and unflappable.

C. Taylor, *Philosophical Arguments*

We become free human beings not by each of us realising ourselves as individuals, according to the hideous phrase, but rather in that we go out of ourselves, enter into relations with others, and in a certain sense relinquish ourselves to them. Only through this process do we determine ourselves as individuals ... more so than someone who, merely to be identical with himself – as though this identity was always desirable – makes a nasty, sour face and gives one to understand from the outset that one does not exist for him and has nothing to contribute to his inwardness, which often enough does not even exist.

T. Adorno, *Critical Models*

Social space is moral space, a point recognized by social theorists from Simmel onwards. However, few theorists have located explanations of everyday behaviour in the interface between technology, cultural values and experience. Earlier chapters have focused upon the ways in which users operationalize forms of asymmetrical behaviour through a variety of strategies embodied in mediated forms of auditized looking. Personal-stereo use appears to reflect a transformation in the rules surrounding forms of everyday social recognition. This poses a question as to the role that personal stereos play in the construction of interpersonal behaviour.

Personal stereos differ from many other forms of communication technology by virtue of their mobility. They also differ from other mobile forms of communication technologies, such as the mobile phone, in as much as mobile phones involve forms of direct inter-personal communication, person to person. The personal-stereo user, in contrast to this, is communing with the products of the culture industry, not individual persons. Personal-stereo use, as has been noted, transforms the nature of the user's representational space. The reception situation becomes identical to the physical embodiment of the user and as such transforms the user's space of reception. The site of reception becomes variously the transformed street, office, bedroom or beach. Just as the placing of the television might be seen to transform the meaning and interactive nature of the domestic interior of the home in a variety of ways, so using a personal stereo transforms and mediates the subject's relation to the environment in ways that require investigation. In this chapter I focus specifically upon interpersonal communicative practices, arguing that personal-stereo use represents a radical re-prioritization of the relation between direct interpersonal communication and technologically mediated experience. Personal-stereo use appears to be situated within an historical and cultural trajectory within which traditional forms of face-to-face commun-ication are increasingly put into competition with technologically simulated forms of experience that are often perceived as being more attractive to users.

In the following pages I analyse the interactive possibilities and consequences of personal stereo practices and situate them within a framework that highlights the management and increasing asymmetrical nature of urban behaviour.

Technology as a Communication Demarcator

'Being-with' a personal stereo is to be absorbed in a continuous flow of sound that acts as an accessory, mediator or constructor of the user's activity. Its use represents a choice, even if it be habitual, of the user's management of their time and space. The act of listening also, necessarily, mediates the realm of the interpersonal by changing the relationship between the user and others. Use permits the user to stop or to ignore communication at any time, with users often evaluating the significance of, or interest of, discourse in relation to use. As such normal discourse is often perceived to be in competition with the heightened quality of personal-stereo use. The following examples are typical:

> If there's a topic of conversation that doesn't interest me then I'll get into my Walkman. (Donna: interview number 52)

> If I like the person or if they say something that interests me I'll switch it off. If not I'll keep it on. If I don't like them I sort of shut out everything that I don't like by putting my Walkman on. (Kim: interview number 25)

> There's people I haven't wanted to speak to; because it's always in my ear and I pretend that its on. But loads of people have said to me that a Walkman's really antisocial. You get hurt at first. When I speak to people I'll take them out of my ear and I'll respect them and try to keep the conversation going as long as I can. But then, if the conversation gets a bit thin and there's silence. Then I'll stick it on again until someone says something. (Jade: interview number 13)

> You can block out noise. If you're not interested in the conversation you can just turn back to your Walkman. You don't have to listen to them. They get the message . . . The other day, he [her father] was complaining about me not doing enough housework. Every week I get the same lecture. I thought. I've had enough of this and I put my Walkman on! Anything that's going on that you get fed up with. You just turn up your music. (Dina: interview number 46)

Users normally dislike being disturbed in the flow of listening. The pleasure derived from use and the planning involved in this mitigates against any unexpected interruption that might destroy the mood-enhancing qualities of listening. Users habitually use strategies of continued listening whilst engaging in interactive processes. The most common being talking with one earphone plugged into the ear thus enabling conversation to continue:

> Or sometimes you can have one in your ear and one out so you can listen to your music as well. (Kayz: interview number 54)

> I take it out of one ear. I listen to music on the phone through head-phones. I listen to the radio through headphones while I'm on the phone. I'll be listening through one ear . . . Because people that phone me like to know what I'm listening to because music's the centre of my world. I couldn't live without music. (Jana: interview number 47)

Through using their personal stereos, users are able to switch off from conversations more easily or they might pretend to be listening, feigning involvement in the conversation. Equally they make judgments as to the level of interest they wish to take in the discourse. The discourse is always in direct competition with the process of consuming personalized sound. Users sense of their self-prioritization is thus enhanced through use, as is the power of disengagement. This can take many forms as exemplified above; users might pick up their personal stereo and put it on as a way of making it obvious to the 'other' that they are not being listened to or to signify the end of the dialogue. Alternatively the personal stereo might be turned up or the body language of the user might be used to signify that the music is of more interest to the user than is the discourse.

Personal stereos can also be used to avoid contact altogether. This is achieved by the user representing themselves as being totally absorbed in listening, thus making it difficult to be interrupted. Alternatively the user might acknowledge the other whilst signifying being otherwise engaged, thus playing on the taken for granted or everyday notion of privacy made visible through use:

> When I'm with people [on the bus]. Yeh. I find myself sitting on the bus. I can't be bothered to talk so you listen to the Walkman . . . if I see people [whilst shopping] that I don't want to talk to, it's a bit rude, but you just turn your Walkman up louder and walk with your head a bit down. (Claire: interview number 48)

There might be someone on the bus I don't particularly want to talk to. So if you have your Walkman on you can smile at them but you don't have to communicate with them. I do that quite a lot. It's an excuse not to talk to somebody. (Amber: interview number 28)

The use of a personal stereo appears to provide a new range of public contexts for the prioritizing of subjective experience. However, this prioritization is not always well received:

This weekend I went to Scotland with my boyfriend and he brought his Walkman. I didn't really mind but he wore them most of the way. I thought it would be nice just to talk or something. I sat there twiddling my thumbs. Once I realized how boring the journey was I didn't mind. (Claire: interview number 48)

Yet whilst the recipient describes being put out by the relegation of her discourse she nevertheless agrees that using a personal stereo is probably of more interest. The use of the personal stereo as an accompaniment for discourse becomes an everyday and normal practice for many users. In the following example Alice, a seventeen-year-old student, accepts the activity of her boyfriend as being normal whilst not necessarily liking it:

If he comes round to my house and he just walks around he often has it on and he'll sit there for quite a long time with one ear, cause he's got the ear plug on . . . and he'll turn the volume down lower. (Alice: interview number 6)

However, the point I wish to stress here is the prioritizing and asymmetrical aspect of use in the normal pattern of interpersonal discourse. It is also significant that in the above examples that relate to a more domestic use, males use personal stereos to prioritize their experience over the woman, thus replicating general male predispositions to prioritize their experience (Morley 1992). When use takes place in interpersonal domestic situations its use becomes more gender stereotypical. One female respondent reported having a difficult domestic situation with her partner, who would invariably walk around the house listening to sports programmes on his personal stereo, thus avoiding what she perceived to be direct discourse with her. This resulted in verbally and sometimes physically violent behaviour between them.

It becomes common practice among users to be simultaneously involved in listening and talking. The following example takes place in a car with the user listening to his personal stereo:

> It's usually at a level where I can listen to music and can still listen to them. This morning the car radio was on and I had my Walkman on and someone else was speaking to me in the front. It was a bit hard trying to converse with the person but I managed it. (Jade: interview number 13)

Users sometimes express social discomfort when enacting their activities of prioritization. The following user dislikes being subject to the prioritising process engaged in by other users:

> Yeh. Because when you see people listening to their Walkman you think they're in their own little world. It's quite antisocial. If you're on a bus with friends and somebody gets a Walkman out. Your company's not good enough! My friends do that. It's really rude. (Rebecca: interview number 49)

This awareness leads some users to switch off or take off their personal stereos when they engage in any form of interactive discourse. Some users feel a sense of discomfort if they are not fully engaged in the process of interaction. Equally, others involved in discourse with users can find the practice threatening to their own sense of significance. The following is a description of use in a college common room:

> My friends do [use the Walkman] when I'm talking to them. But I personally can't stand it when somebody does it to me. So I don't do it to others. It's all to do with. If I'm talking to someone, even though I know they can be listening to me. I always feel they they're not really interested. You can at least have the common courtesy to turn it off when I'm talking to you. It's not even that. It's the fact that a lot of people have one ear in and then they'll say you're not really listening to it and you know they're listening to it and they insist on lying to you. (John: interview number 20)

Personal-stereo use thus remains a visible sign of the threat to the significance of the 'other' in everyday patterns of social discourse. Through its prioritizing of the subject its use creates an implicit competition between non-mediated interpersonal discourse and the mediated sounds of the culture industry. The use of personal stereos can be seen in the above examples as typifying the asymmetry built into forms of everyday patterns of discourse which are enhanced by communication technologies such as personal stereos.

Strategies for Avoiding Verbal Contact: Personal Stereos as Conversational Preserves

Other aspects of interpersonal behaviour mediated through the use of personal stereos appear to be consonant with accounts of urban spaces as places of incipient danger or insecurity. Whilst most of the examples discussed up to now have showed how people use personal stereos to navigate through public space in isolation and has dealt with their attitude towards 'others' as a backcloth to their own private somnamb-ulations, the present section will deal with how people use them to fend off unwanted or threatening interruption.

Personal stereos, as noted previously, can be used as a form of 'conversational preserve'. Goffman used this phrase to define the ability of a person to exert some control over who talks in public and when. Personal stereos are a tool enabling the individual to manoeuvre through urban spaces without coming into direct contact with other people. Both the artifact and the resultant strategies of 'looking' create this 'conversational preserve'. The communality of urban experience is juxtaposed with the co-presence of something unique to the user which is the individual control of their own choice of sounds marking them off from any communal experience beyond them. Goffman was already indicating in 1971 the existence of a crumbling edifice of urban public civility in his discussion of the latent insecurities underlying common forms of public inattention.

> The vulnerability of public life is what we're coming more and more to see. Certainly in the great public forums of our society, the downtown areas of our cities, can come to be uneasy places. Militantly sustained antagonisms between diffusely intermingled major population segments – young and old, male and female, white and black, impoverished and well off – can cause those in public gatherings to distrust (and to fear they are distrusted by) the person standing next to them. The forms of civil inattention of persons circumspectly treating one another with polite and glancing concern while each goes about his separate business, may be maintained, but behind these normal appearances individuals can come to be at the ready, poised to flee or to fight back if necessary and

in place of unconcern there can be alarm – until, that is, the streets are redefined as naturally precarious places, and a high level of risk becomes routine. (Goffman 1971, p. 386)

Goffman's theme is discussed here with specific reference to the gendering of urban spaces. Concerns of security and feelings of apprehension in public are most commonly, but not exclusively, expressed by women. Such a concern is engendered in aspects of use enabling the user to operationalize a range of strategies that create feelings of security in them. Whilst not all women interviewed used personal stereos thus, many respondents mentioned the possibility of this type of use. This is not to say that only women experience the city as at times threatening but merely that they expressed these feeling more often. Males users virtually never used or admitted using their personal stereo's as a response to any perceived or imagined threat in public although do describe using them, like female users, as a controller of interaction. Female users describe using the personal stereo as a barrier to discourse in which the use of it represents a sign that the user is 'somewhere else' or 'fully occupied'. It performs the same role as a 'do not disturb' sign:

Also I use it as an excuse if I'm worried about the person I'm sitting next to. Often I'll put the earphones in and wont turn it on so that I'm aware of what's going on. If there's a drunk on the train I'll put the earphones in and appear to be blank and they won't bother you. (Catriona: interview number 14)

Use functions as a form of security in this situation. It is coupled with the awareness that the actual use of a personal stereo could be counter-productive as the loss of hearing might constitute a potential vulnerability in terms of the perceived position of threat. Other users continue to play music but reduce the volume, or might keep their fingers on the volume control of their personal stereo:

I always have it in my pocket and I have my finger on the volume and then I see something, or see a car or something. I turn it down and listen and I turn it back up again when I feel I'm on familiar territory. (Betty: interview number 34)

In contexts where the woman feels attention is unwanted or threatening the personal stereo becomes a useful prop facilitating the creation of a conversational preserve as the following example of a woman walking home late at night demonstrates:

> I sometimes use the Walkman, say at 3.00. a.m. Say I get a night bus and walk home from there and the road's deserted and you walk home and you don't get bothered. But when I walk home when the pubs are turned out and you get all these people saying. 'Óh darling, bla, bla, bla!' And I say: 'Sorry, I can't hear you. I'm listening!' And I walk on past and that would fool them. They don't know what to say. That's a really good trick. They won't ask you twice. (Mags: interview number 31)

Unwanted interruption or perceived threat is not limited to the pavement or tube but can also be encountered whilst riding a bicycle. The following example demonstrate the fear of a woman whilst riding around the city at night:

> At that time of night I'm not really happy about cycling. I would probably even take a cab with my bike. So it [her Walkman] does stop me from doing that . . . The other reason I have it on loud is sometimes on the road you get shouted at on the bike by people, like in cars and things and, so, that way you can block it out. You just get it a lot . . . General things. Just shouting. Sexual things. I block it all out. Sometimes they drive up along you and slow down and be saying things to you and so you turn around and it can be really dangerous. And so in a way I think it's less dangerous for me having the Walkman actually because I don't turn when people are shouting . . . Some of my friends have been dragged off their bikes. (Dorinda: interview number 32)

This woman feels a greater sense of security through using her personal stereo because it acts both as a barrier between her and any unwanted contact with other drivers and also because the music she plays on it makes her feel more confident. In this instance the playing of a familiar tape creates a sense of security in her. The following user who is also a cyclist responds more aggressively as the music in this case acts as a trigger to a more assertive response:

> There are some people. They can see you're wearing a Walkman. They pick on you. Well I can hear them! 'You asshole. You know I can hear what you're saying. I'm not a lip reader. Now shut the fuck up and let me listen to my music! I can hear.' Sometimes I deliberately ignore them. (Robina: interview number 35)

The use of a personal stereo to avoid unwanted attention does not, however, work in all circumstances:

> Sometimes. When you're on the tube with it and you'll be listening to it and someone will ask you where's the train going. And you won't know what they're saying. You'll have to stop and say: 'What? I can't hear you!' And you think why don't they ask the person next to you. I'm busy and I don't want to be disturbed! It's a bit irritating. You stop. You're really into this piece of music and you have to stop it, turn the volume down. stop and say. 'What did you say?' (Mags: interview number 31)

Other users are more sceptical as to the efficacy of personal stereos as a form of conversational preserve:

> There are certain people that if they want to talk they'll talk to you even if you've got your Walkman. They force you to take it off. So I never think about that [using it in this way]. (Karin: interview number 18)

At other times users do not so much respond to specific intrusions as merely to a feeling of potential danger or threat which personal-stereo use alleviates:

> You don't take notice of anyone with it on. I don't care. Whereas if I haven't got it on. Because everything seems different if you're used to getting there with music in your ears. You can hear other people [without the Walkman]. If you hear them. You're watching them. There's more paranoia without it. (Sara: interview number 50)

This non attention constitutes a blocking out of apprehension and leads some women to use it in circumstances they might otherwise feel was potentially unsafe. The personal stereo becomes their companion in these circumstances:

> When I'm walking along with my Walkman I can never tell if anyone's behind me . . . [the Walkman]. It's like company. (Jana: interview number 47)

The paradoxical situation whereby using a personal stereo produces an artificial sense of security whilst in effect making the user more vulnerable is captured in the following account:

It's strange. I'm a lot more alert because I know – This is another horrible thing. But I remember someone getting raped several years ago because. It was quite dark. She had her Walkman on. Didn't hear him. And I thought. 'Bloody stupid cow. I would never do that!' But I do it. um. But it's like, obviously I don't have it on as loud. But I'm a lot more aware when I've got it on . . . I'm looking now, um, because it's like. Shit! Here I am. It's ten o' clock. It's dark and I've got my Walkman on. So. It's like I know it's stupid. So there's this little thing goes off in my head that says. 'I'm on Betty alert!' Because I know I shouldn't have it on . . . I feel secure but insecure . . . I feel safe with the music, but I feel what's around me for the very first time you could really say. (Betty: interview number 34)

The music, in this description, functions as a personalized form of security adjusting the senses whereby the awareness of the outside world becomes heightened and is given presence despite the sound of the music in the user's head. This heightened sense of her surroundings leads the following user to adjust the volume if necessary:

If I see somebody or someone's walking behind me. I'll switch it off so I could hear. So I'm completely back. Non of this half-hearted business. I'm completely back until I've made myself a little secure. (Betty: interview number 34)

It appears that users can operate an overdrive system of the senses which enable them to readjust to the world outside of them. However, this subjective feeling of control is often contradicted by those users who have had their conversational preserves threatened. The following account by a 32-year-old female radio producer is worth quoting in full:

There was a time not very long ago. I live in Brixton and I was walking, during the day to the overground station and much later than I would have done otherwise I realised there was a bloke coming towards me, clearly off his head, with a baseball bat, looking with some intent to do some odd, mad thing with it. He really was very near to me when I bolted . . . and there's something about, you have to stop the sound. I find I can't react to what's happening unless I switch it off. There's a lot of me trying to run away but then thinking. Don't be ridiculous! Move away from that person quickly. I find I can't, I can't just take the earphones out and let the thing carry on. If someone asks me for a light or directions I'll have to root around, find it, Switch it off . . . There was an alarmed feeling of it being, of being in this other world, having this musical experience has meant that I haven't had my third eye available to sense what's going on around me . . . and once there is that realization that there's something happening. It's like: Get out of this now. All at once you need to be right back in there, with all guns blazing, hearing what he might be saying. Somehow it seems more important to come immediately back into the situation rather than get out of it staying in there [keeping the Walkman on]. It's a panic of all things at once . . . It didn't make me aware of where I was with the music. It's when you come crashing back into that other world. It seems different from when you left it. It seemed, sort of fluorescent with this strange behaviour I was receiving. (Jo: interview number 30)

The difficulty of switching to an appropriate mode of reaction whilst being absorbed in a private world of auditory experience is apparent from the above description. The movement from one soundworld to another is invariably hindered with the user having to switch the personal stereo off before responding adequately to the situation. This slowness of response to unexpected situations appears to be a common experience amongst users.

The above examples demonstrate how the use of a personal stereo may create feelings of security amongst female users in specific situations. This is not to imply that this is the prime motivation for use amongst women as it most clearly is not. The use of a personal stereo can construct conversational preserves and constitute boundary markers in many situations permitting the user to transcend the perceived insecurity of urban movement. In doing so they enable the user to transcend, in part, the gendered spaces of the city.

Sharing your Personal Stereo

Whilst most use of personal stereos is solitary, they can be used to frame forms of collective use. Usually joint or collective use takes place amongst teenage users. Personal stereos provides some users with interactive possibilities in their mundane everyday use that isn't replicated amongst other users whose use of personal stereos is generally more prescribed. There is a variation in the structure of use amongst adults (largely for commuting or sports activities) as against teenagers (everyday experience saturated with music). The sites of collective use are invariably school common rooms, the school bus and so on.

However, whilst keeping this distinction in mind, this study is not aimed at providing a youth subcultural account of use but rather to elaborate upon a more structural phenomenology of use.

Personal stereos have a facility for shared listening. It is possible either to share the headsets, one earpiece per person or alternatively some machines have an extension socket enabling two sets of headphones to be used. Sharing normally takes the form of two people listening to the same music at the same time. This differs from users who listen to their own personal stereos and swap tapes between them. Listening in groups of two can also be part of a wider listening scenario where several groups of users are together. Users, if they do share, invariably intersperse listening with talking. This transforms talk which assumes more an air of visibility and of display as the speech is loud in order to overcome the parallel sound of the music. Conversation is thus accompanied by and interspersed by music:

> You share. You have it in one ear. The other person has the other ear and you just blast it . . . [it] livens up the conversation because one minute you're talking the next minute you're singing lyrics out. (Dina: interview number 46)

The headphones stay in and the performance continues. For these sixteen-year-old users listening to music through their personal stereos whilst interacting makes them more enervated with their discussion becoming more exited as it is buoyed on by the accompanying music. Conversation and behaviour also becomes more public and consequently one aspect of their behaviour becomes display or alternatively, refers to the inconsequentiality of the social world beyond them. Listening also facilitates the continuation of their interaction making it easier to maintain over time. The music acts as an accompaniment filling in the gaps in speech thus abolishing any pregnant pauses that might otherwise occur. The music itself can also provide a topic of conversation if necessary:

> If by chance we run out of things to say then we start singing to the song or comment on how wicked the song is or how beautiful it is. then we start arguing! (Dina: interview number 46)

> I like listening to my Walkman with someone else because you can share the experience. Someone will be saying; 'that's a nice song', and you'll sit there and have a meaningful discussion about it. Sometimes you don't

want to not listen to your Walkman so you'll share it [in the common room]. (Jana: interview number 47)

Personal stereo's can be shared by peers on the way to school, on the bus, in the school common room or in corridors whilst waiting for lessons to begin. These areas become listening posts for users and a way of demarcating one group off from others. Often the demarcation line is understood in terms of the type of music listened to. However, some users use their personal stereos in order to keep a distance from others, as not all use is collective in these environments. The social or communal feature of use is described below by the following seventeen-year-old students:

Other people. They start joining in. (Zoe: interview number 53)

If you're listening to your Walkman you always have someone there, 'uh, uh, Can I listen to it?' (Sarah: interview number 51)

In the common room everyone's in their own world. Everyone's got their Walkman in their ear. Doing things. They don't really care. They play cards with their Walkman. All you can hear them shouting is 'Is it my turn!' . . . It's amazingly loud in the common room, It [Walkman listening] does sort of block out the rest of the noise. (Kayz: interview number 54)

Groups mill around with some focused on listening whilst others intersperse listening with playing. The common room is divided by gender and/or ethnicity together with musical taste, with musical taste tending to function as a form of public exclusivity between the groups, as the following sixteen- year-olds describe:

Normally in the common room people sit in tens. We all sit together. Some people have their personal stereos on but not everybody. (Anne: interview number 4)

I never listen to my Walkman on my own in college. In the common room most of us have personal stereos and so we like to share. Today I shared with a friend of mine. This happens everyday. We just listen. We were having a conversation and it was hard to hear what he was saying . . . There's a large group. Sixteen to twenty people. Today my friend played me something. It was live so I asked him what it was . . . I enjoy sitting in the common room. Everybody together. That's the only time I see everyone. (Alice: interview number 6)

Many teenage users like to share their personal stereos at strategic times of the day. Use becomes both a means whereby you can advertise the significance of your musical taste and a form of passing time in a 'heightened' manner. It becomes a way of maintaining dialogue in an acceptable form. Not all teenage users like to share, however. Many still perceive it as a private or personal affair or see their musical taste as being unique to them.

Personal stereos can be used jointly or collectively in many social situations. The following is a description of teenage users going out on a Saturday night:

> If you're travelling with someone and there's two of you. If there's a lot of you and you're going somewhere and lots of people are talking and you just want to not bother and you just sit back and listen to the Walkman with someone else. What often happens if we're going to a club. There's lots of us and there's people sitting opposite you and in a long line all with personal stereos. We do that a lot. (Isobel: interview number 26)

The above is consonant with the perceived need to have experience either accompanied to, or constituted by music. The use of personal stereos in these situations also represents 'something going on'. A heightening of the normal mundane situation that users find themselves in. It can also be perceived to reflect on the social status of the user. Teenagers are virtually universally imbued with music culture which forms a central role in their speech, dress, leisure and friendships and social projection. (Thornton 1995) Personal stereo use represents a continuation of this, permitting status through musical taste to be expressed in an active way at times when it would otherwise be difficult to express.

Adults share their personal stereos much more rarely. On those occasions when they do there is a perceived air of deviancy or performance attached to it. This is coupled to an understanding of its representational meaning in the social field. The following two examples are typical. Both users are in their late twenties, the first female, the second male:

> It was basically a beach holiday and we were on our own together the whole time. For both of us, everyday at different times. I'd be quite surprised when her Walkman hour would come before mine. It was like being hungry before me. Too early for me. The only time we danced the

whole holiday. It wasn't a dancy resort. We had one dance with our duo dock thing, um, just on our patio. This frantic dance to a Bjork track. It was excellent. We both had the headphones on and I was holding my Walkman. It was brilliant because it was so internalized and we knew we were making a noise and laughing and kind of . . . I just love the idea of what people over the wall will have heard; shuffling and gigglings and things. It was great. (Jo: interview number 30)

The above example highlights a feeling of exclusivity of experience. The music binds the users together through the dance that is theirs alone. They are aware of their acoustic specialness and imagine the ears of others hearing the results of their movements and actions as deviant actions. Deviant, because of the lack of music, bodily sound substituting for visual presence. The following example differs from this as it is primarily visual. What unites both examples is the perceived deviancy of the public display, visual or not, of joint use. Both sets of users are aware of potential public disapproval:

We've walked out of the pub down the local high street and we've both got the headphones. We've got the two headphones in one Walkman. Just for a laugh we go dancing down the high street. People are just looking at us. 'What's going on?' Purely for a laugh in the local village. They're used to us now. I've lived there for ten years. It amuses us you know. We'll sit in the bus stop and our arms are going up. All those straight faces! People say it's like an act rather than shocking. It's entertaining. It's a performance. The High Street on stage. (Ben: interview number 41)

Personal-stereo use can thus produce a collective bubble that distinguishes users from non-users. This chapter has indicated the ways in which personal stereos provide users with a range of strategic possibilities for instrumentalizing forms of interpersonal behaviour and operationalizing a range of asymmetrical interpersonal strategies of urban behaviour. It has also pointed to the role and significance of personal stereos in providing a continual accompaniment to the everyday experience of users. In doing so the chapter sheds light on the relational nature of a technologically mediated interpersonal environment in which users habitually prioritize their experience.

Part III

Personal Steroes and a Critical Theory of Urban Everyday Life

Sounding Out the City: An Auditory Epistemology of Urban Experience

The city is increasingly the technological site of human habitation, the place where the collision of technology and the human spirit is most marked.

H. Caygill, *Walter Benjamin*

Every sense delivers contributions characteristic of its individual nature to the construction of sociated existence; peculiarities of the social relationship correspond to the nuancing of its impressions; the prevalence of one or the other sense in the contact of individuals often provides this contact with a sociological nuance that could otherwise not be produced.

G. Simmel, *The Sociology of the Senses*

I suppose you could say it's [the personal stereo] part of my body. I've got a special pocket for it. It's got its home. It's been a therapy putting it on outside. Because I'm rushing out, doing something. It's an important part of relaxation. Because what I've been doing is something visual. Sound is something else. You feel it's slower, slower than light. You hear things not just through your eardrums but through your whole body. Your whole body is vibrating. I suppose it cancels out the vibrations of the traffic around you. If energy is going in through your ear it vibrates all of your bones, every single bone in your body. You're moving. You've got energy inside you. It's in you. You're not just hearing it.

Karin: interview number 18

The phenomenological analysis of personal-stereo use presented in the previous chapters points to the critical need of developing an auditory

115

epistemology of everyday urban life. Visually based explanations of everyday life are dominated by subjects merely responding to the external stimuli of the city framed within a theoretical dualism in which subjects are portrayed either as actively or passively engaging with their surroundings. Yet, without an understanding of the significance of forms of auditory experience as highlighted in the previous chapters, we are unable to adequately analyse the relational qualities attached to the daily experience of personal-stereo users.

In this chapter I develop an auditory epistemology of urban experience that addresses the above issues before going on to outline a critical theory of urban space and habitation. Urban space is filled with sounds. A letter from a professor of music complains of the intrusive bass sounds emanating from passing cars that penetrate his double-glazed study. Others complain about the intrusive television sounds coming from hard-of-hearing neighbours. Sound is no respecter of 'private' space as it is multiple and amorphous. The audible is intangible, unlike vision which more often than not focuses upon objects. The relational qualities of the two senses are completely different. Yet the analysis of urban experience through the sense of vision has been the predominant one in urban and cultural studies. Simmel, for example, whilst having addressed the nature of urban sound in describing Berlin at the turn of the century, has nevertheless become a seminal influences upon a generation of later urbanists who refer to him as having created the definitive visual paradigm of urban relations. His awareness of and discussion of the nature of the auditative in relation to the visual tends to be overlooked by most commentators. Yet an auditory investigation of experience produces a very different picture of urban experience, demonstrating the inappropriateness of studying the auditative through a visual lens. Kahn aptly illustrates the problem:

> How . . . can listening be explained when the subject in recent theory has been situated, no matter how askew, in the web of the gaze, mirroring, reflection, the spectacle, and other ocular tropes? Visually disposed language, furthermore, favours thinking about sound as an object, but sound functions poorly in this regard: It dissipates, modulates, infiltrates other sounds, becomes absorbed and deflected by actual objects, and fills space surrounding them. (Kahn and Whitehead 1992, p. 4)

Sound differs from vision in its relational qualities and in the placing and spacing of experience. Of course, cultures are both auditive and visual, and none of the following remarks are meant to discount the visual nature of urban experience but rather serve to locate the auditory within the matrix of urban experience. The sensory environment of the city, just as the habitual way in which we look, hear and experience, is closely tied to recent technological developments that inform and are informed by a set of western cultural values ranging from individualism, privatization to forms of everyday 'instrumentalism'. The personal stereo is merely a recent technological addition permitting the management of experience through these cultural imperatives. Yet whilst the role of the camera in the transformation of experience has often been discussed, less attention has been paid to sound. The rise of the radio in the 1920s, sound accompaniment to film or the rise of mechanically reproduced music through records have taken a back seat to explanations that prioritize the visual in everyday experience. These explanations ignore the specific relational components of auditory experience. Grivel points to the relational qualities of sound in the sense of its differing presence within the subject, whilst also pointing to the potentially utopian or 'magical' quality of the machine itself – a theme I take up later through the work of Adorno. The machine as such, discloses the desire of the user:

> A phonograph seduces doubly every time: it fulfils its little nasal function and roots me in reality as I cannot imagine. It reproduces and it symbolises, the one with the other, the one inside the other, inseparable . . . A machine corresponds necessarily to a call of the imaginary . . . a machine corresponds to what the user expects of it but also provides him with an unprecedented, unformulated response of which itself is the idea. (Grivel 1992, p. 35)

The ability of sound to transform the relationship between the receiver and the source of information is important to the present analysis of personal-stereo use. As such, my analysis of personal-stereo use has drawn our attention to the multifaceted transformation of urban experience through the auditory. Welsch has recently noted the differing temporal relationship to experience that the auditory has as compared with the visual:

> the mode of being of the visible and audible is fundamentally different. The visible persists in time, the audible, however vanished in time. Vision is concerned with constant, enduring being, audition on the other hand, with the fleeting, the transient, event like. (Welsch 1997, p. 157)

Vision thus attempts to impose order upon flux by attempting to fix objects, whilst sound is transitory. Connor mentions the specific nature of auditory experience in terms of:

> its capacity to disintegrate and reconfigure space . . . Where auditory experience is dominant, we may say, singular perspectival gives way to plural permeated space. The self defined in terms of hearing rather than sight is a self imaged not as a point, but as a membrane; not as a picture, but as a channel through which voices, noises and musics travel . . . sound is omnipresent, non directional and mobile. (Connor 1997, pp. 206–7)

Auditive experience is described as being more decentred or despatialized than visual experience in the above examples. However, this is far too simple. I have demonstrated in the previous chapters a variety of user strategies in which sound becomes a medium for the production of forms of centredness through the reconstruction of narrative and place. This demonstrates the pitfalls of relying upon an abstract analysis of personal-stereo use tied to a rudimentary understanding of the auditory, as this might indeed lead to the assertion of decentred and despatialized experience, as in the work of Hosokawa and Chambers. This clearly demonstrates the need to relate everyday experience empirically and historically to appropriate theoretical categories. For example, a disembodied analysis of sound would indeed focus upon its amorphous nature, whereas my detailed ethnography of personal-stereo use points to a set of contrary conclusions.

For example, users often use their personal stereos continually to 'repeat' experience through the repetition of chosen sounds. This suspension of time and management of mood through sound is contrary to accepted wisdom concerning the social meanings attached to forms of auditory cognition. Welsch, for example, draws the following distinctions between the auditative and the visual, stating that:

> In vision the world congeals into objects . . . It is completely different with hearing, which does not reduce the world to distance, but rather accommodates it. Whereas vision is a distancing sense, hearing is one of alliance . . . hearing . . . does not keep the world at a distance, but admits it. 'Tone penetrates, without distance.' Such penetration, vulnerability and exposure are characteristic of hearing. We have eyelids, but not earlids. In hearing we are unprotected. Hearing is a sense of extreme passivity, and we cannot escape from acoustic congestion. – That is why we are especially in need of protection acoustically. (Welsch 1997, p. 158)

These observations are problematic if applied to personal-stereo use. Welsch argues that the ears are unprotected and unable to distance themselves from the world, and thereby they passively attend to it. Personal-stereo use, however, demonstrates the historical specificity of this assumption. Personal stereos can rather be seen as technologically empowering the subject. The headphones enclose the ears and substitute chosen and specific sound for the industrialized, fordist and acoustically congested sounds of the street. Paradoxically, personal stereos can act as a form of acoustic protection for the user. This awareness of the specific nature of auditory experience is not sufficient without an adequate understanding of the historical and cultural make up of those sensory experiences.

Simmel, usefully, attributes both a cognitive and a moral status to the senses, and in doing so his work provides some useful indications as to how an analysis of personal-stereo use might proceed. Simmel perceives the auditory as being simultaneously egotistical and democratic. By egotism Simmel refers to the ears as drawing everything into them but as having no power of choice over what they take in. Thus the democratic nature of the auditory lies precisely in this lack of discrimination. This indifference also alludes to an alternative form of spatiality and relatedness in the nature of the auditory:

> One can possess only the 'visible' whereas that which is only audible is already past in the moment of its present and provides no 'property' . . . hearing is by its very nature supra individual; what happens in a room must be heard by all those present there, and the fact that one person receives it does not deprive another of it. (Simmel 1997b, pp. 115–16)

The possessive nature of the auditory differs from the visual, according to Simmel, inasmuch as sound is not appropriated in the same way as the visual. It also, significantly, has different temporal qualities:

> The ear transmits the wealth of divergent moods of individuals, the flow and the momentary external expression of thoughts and impulses, the entire polarity of subjective as well as objective life. (Simmel 1997b, p. 117)

The auditory, in Simmel's account, is multiple, thus producing instability and vulnerability in the subject, whereas the visual is more linear and unambiguous. Simmel describes the urban dweller as being flooded by the auditory whilst also being visually invaded by the 'look' of others. The result is that, throughout the modern era, the quest of the individual is for his self, for a fixed and unambiguous point of reference. He needs such a fixed point more and more urgently in view of the unprecedented expansion of theoretical and practical perspectives and the complication of life, and the related fact that he can no longer find it anywhere outside himself. (Simmel 1971a, p. 175)

Thus the auditative, importantly, imposes a different structure upon the nature of interpersonal relations in relation to the visual. The auditative is described as procedural whereas the 'look' is described in terms of simultaneousness. If we take Simmel's account into consideration, the auditory might appear to open up the possibility of forms of asymmetry dissimilar to those produced through the dynamic of the 'look'. The relational quality of auditory looking could well differ from that of non-auditory 'looking'. Simmel's theory of urban experience thus incorporates important insights into the nature of the auditative whilst underplaying the historical constitution of those senses, a point rectified in the early work of The Frankfurt School.

Critical Theory and the Historical Configuration of the Senses

Critical Theory's contribution to an understanding of the organization of senses in relation to technology has been largely neglected. Yet their work provides a sophisticated theoretical framework for understanding such behaviour. Critical Theorists recognized the historical constitution of the senses which became central to their evaluation of the relationship between agency and social structure. Within the context of an historically constituted sensory 'self', forms of representational space together with the manner in which subjects construct their horizon of experience become intimately tied to the social formation and organization of the senses. Therefore, notions of 'looking', 'seeing', 'remembering' and 'hearing' become mediated cultural practices and strategies, as indeed does the very constitution of 'experience'. Horkheimer makes this point in an early essay:

The objects we perceive in our surroundings – cities, villages, fields and woods – bear the mark of having been worked on by man. It is not only in clothing and appearance, in outward form and emotional make up that men are the products of history. Even the way they see and hear is inseparable from the social life process as it has evolved over the millennia.

The facts which our senses present to us are socially pre- formed in two ways: through the historical character of the object perceived and through the historical character of the perceiving organ. (Horkheimer 1972, p. 200)

The organisation of the senses are perceived of as being inherently fluid by Horkheimer, a position supported throughout the writings of other Critical Theorists. This insight is developed in the present study by investigating the ways in which the use of personal stereos reorganizes the senses so as to prioritize the auditory over the visual.

The early work of Critical Theorists investigated the transformation of sensory experience within the urban through an analysis of new forms of communication technology. (Adorno 1941a, b and c, 1990a; Benjamin 1973b) Benjamin makes the following observation in relation to film and experience:

Within broad historical epochs the mode of sense perception changes with the overall mode of being in the world of the historical collective. (Benjamin 1973b, p. 224)

This neglected aspect of their work is commented upon by Howard Caygill where he states in relation to perception that:

Benjamin underlines this claim for the epochal character of perception by adding that 'the manner in which perception is organised, the medium in which it is accomplished' is not only natural, but determined by 'historical circumstances as well . . . He proposes to go further and investigate 'the social transformations expressed by these changes of perception.' (Caygill 1998, p104)

This point goes to the centre of Critical Theorists' work on communication and technology, in which Benjamin discusses the transformation of visuality and Adorno discusses the transformation of the auditory. The context within which this is discussed incorporates an understanding of the construction of the site of experience within a transformed and reconstituted public and private sphere. Critical Theorists gave technology a central role in the construction and transformation of the cognitive, aesthetic and moral 'spacings' of everyday experience. They perceived the spaces of the city to be the increasingly mediated and saturated by new forms of communication technologies. These processes, they argued, informed the very construction of subjective horizons of experience. The site of experience is thus tied to larger social forces that incorporate the very cultural meanings inscribed in the development and production of communication artifacts and the attendant modes of consumption associated with them, as in the realm of cinema, radio, music and, later, television. Critical Theorists were particularly attentive to changes in the constitution of the social wherein the constitution of the 'knowing subject', both in terms of cognition and in their horizon of experience, lies increasingly in social forms existing beyond the individual experiencing subject. Technology thus becomes central both in terms of the constitution of, and as the object of, volition. Experience is thus increasingly perceived as technological experience in their analysis of the urban.

Technology, the Senses and Spaces of Habitation

Adorno's analysis of the auditory represents the urban subject as not so much protecting the site of experience from others as creating, albeit ambiguously, a utopian space of habitation. The fragility of this space is rendered more secure as the space becomes 'occupied' by signifiers of an imaginary and reassuring presence. Through a close reading of Adorno's work one can find this process described somewhat unsystematically as a state of 'being with' or 'we-ness' by which Adorno refers to the substitution of direct experience by technologically mediated forms of experience. This term refers to a qualitative relationship between the subject and that which is experienced. Indifference to the social, as highlighted in the work of Sennett (1990), is a qualitative stance which in Adorno's account of urban experience becomes a structural response, not merely to confusion but also to a transformation of the subjects relation to the social network. Within this transformation the role of music or sound is prioritized. Adorno argues that music:

> takes the place of the utopia it promises. By circling people, by enveloping them – as inherent in the acoustical phenomenon – and turning them as listeners into participants, it contributes ideologically to the integration which modern society never tires of achieving in reality. It leaves no room for conceptual reflection between itself and the subject, and so it creates an illusion of immediacy in the totally mediated world, a proximity between strangers, of warmth for those who come to feel the chill of the unmitigated struggle of all against all. Most important among

the functions of consumed music – which keeps evoking memories of a language of immediacy – may be that it eases men's suffering under the universal mediations, as if one were still living face to face in spite of it all. (Adorno 1976a, p. 46)

Without necessarily endorsing the implied totalitarian nature of technology in the above quote, Adorno's insight is significant in its highlighting of the auratic quality of music together with its integrative and utopian function. Adorno describes, importantly for my purposes, issues of cognition, aesthetics and the interpersonal. The subjective desire to transcend the everyday through music becomes a focal point of his analysis, as is the desire to remain 'connected' to specific cultural products. The nature of this 'connection' constitutes the state of 'we-ness' which also provides the 'subjective' moment in Adorno's analysis of music reception. The 'social' undergoes a transformation through the colonization of representational space by forms of communication technology, and the 'site' of experience is subsequently transformed thus changing the subject's 'interiority'. This 'transformation' is replicated phenomenologically in the behaviour of personal-stereo users in their everyday experience. States of 'we-ness' thus might be seen dialectically as colonizing the user's desire for social attachment, thereby creating new forms of experiential dependency within the emancipatory desires of the user. Personal-stereo users experience an immediacy and intimacy similar to that described by Adorno in which auditory forms of experience also become auratic. The status of this auratic transformation of experience will be discussed a little later on in the chapter.

The Role of the Auditory in the Creation of States of 'We-Ness'

Roughly speaking, all music, including the most 'objective' and non expressive, belongs primarily to the sphere of subjective inwardness, whereas even the most spiritual of painting is heavily burdened with unresolved objectivity. (Adorno and Eisler 1994, p. 71)

In Adorno's work the relationship between the auditory and states of 'we-ness' is intimate. Adorno perceives acoustic perception to be 'archaic' and pre-individualistic, embodying the memory and anticipation of a collective state.

The fact that music as a whole, and polyphony in particular – the necessary medium of modern music – have their source in the collective practices of cult and dance is not to be written off as a mere 'point of departure' due to its progress towards freedom. Rather this historical source remains the unique sensory subjective impulse in music, even if it has long since broken with every collective practice. Polyphonic music says 'we' even when it lives as a conception only in the mind of the composer, otherwise reaching no living being. The ideal collectivity still contained within music, even though it has lost its relationship to the empirical collectivity, leads inevitably to conflict because of its unavoidable social isolation. Collective perception is the basis of musical objectification itself, and when the latter is no longer possible, it is necessarily degraded almost to a fiction – to the arrogance of the aesthetic subject, which says 'we', while in reality it is still only 'I' – and this 'I' can say nothing at all without positing the 'we'. (Adorno 1973, pp. 18–19)

Music plays a utopian role in the relational aspirations of subjects in Adorno's analysis. Yet he is also sensitive to the changing nature and influence of the auditory within new forms of mechanical reproduction. Adorno perceived music as increasingly filling the spaces of 'habitation' in western culture and in doing so understood that 'the communal, hedonistic, utopian elements of musical perception [are] fetishized [and] put into the service of commercialism' (Adorno and Eisler 1994, p. xxxv). This was particularly the case in film music in which the movie score encouraged forms of emotional proximity. The proximity involved in music reception differs from that involved in perception:

Music is supposed to bring out the spontaneous, essentially human element in its listeners and in virtually all human relations . . . acoustical perception preserves comparably more traits of long bygone, pre-individualistic collectivities than optical perception. (Adorno and Eisler 1994, p. 21)

Within a technologized horizon of experience I understand states of 'we-ness' as being built into both polyphonous music as well as into other forms of representation that involve a combination of the auditory and the visual, such as in soaps, radio chat shows and television news programmes. In analysing the subject's experience thus, experience can be described as being 'auratic'[1] in which the subject's relationship to society undergoes a potential 'monumentalization'.[2] Benjamin's understanding of aura can itself be historicized in order to demonstrate that contemporary forms of mechanical reproduction can work to re-auratize experience in ways not anticipated by Benjamin. Personal-stereo users habitually experience auratic states in their daily listening habits and have a tendency to 'monumentalize' that experience by negating or suspending their experience in the linear time of the everyday.

It was precisely these earlier forms of mechanized production which produced new forms of mediated reception that were of central concern to early Critical Theorists. I interpret these states of 'we-ness' structurally rather than prescriptively, thereby not implying a uniform set of responses amongst users.[3] Personal stereo users have been demonstrated as drawing upon a wide range of creative responses to both sound and environment that precludes a reductivist analysis of their behaviour.

How should we understand the relationship between the site of reception and 'representational' space in this newly configured world of technologized experience? Critical Theorists argued that new forms of technologically orientated communications, such as the radio, prioritized the individual, thereby enhancing forms of existing individualism whilst simultaneously dispelling, substituting or transforming notions of community through the creation of alternative forms of interpersonal communication. These values manifest themselves in the object and its production. This is what is meant by claiming that forms of mobility are inscribed into the meaning and design of the personal stereo. The social relations produced within culture via both technology and individualism act to enhance these self same processes. For this reason the manner in which representation space is transformed through the auditory is of central importance to my analysis of personal-stereo use.

The Auditory, The Relational and Representational Space

I begin my analysis of the relational qualities associated with social space through a discussion of Henri Lefebvre's spatial analysis of urban experience. Lefebvre's work bears a distinct affinity to the early writings of Critical Theorists. If personal-stereo use transforms the relationship between the user and urban space then I locate this relationship conceptually within Lefebvre's understanding of representational space, by which he means:

> Space as directly lived through its associated images and symbols, and hence the space of 'inhabiters' and 'users' . . . This is the dominated –

and hence passively experienced – space which the imagination seeks to change and appropriate. It overlays physical space, making symbolic use of its object . . . Representational space is alive: it speaks. It has an effective kernel or centre: Ego, bed, bedroom, dwelling house; or square, church, graveyard. It embraces the loci of passion, of action and lived situations . . . It may be directional, situational or relational, because it is essentially qualitative, fluid and dynamic. (Lefebvre 1991b, pp. 39–42)

The 'site' of experience exists for Lefebvre within representational space. This can be described phenomenologically in terms of the direction, situation and relation of the experiencing subject. Lefebvre's analysis is able to accommodate a qualitative, multilayered and dynamic evaluation of experience in relation to its surroundings. However, in doing so Lefebvre appears to create an either/or dichotomy that sits uneasily with his otherwise fluid analysis of experience. He claims that lived space is passively experienced as a 'given' with the imaginary or symbolic activity of the individual appearing to be fully colonized by saturated forms of representational space:

> Living bodies, the bodies of 'users' – are caught up not only in the toils of parcelised space, but also in the web of what philosophers call 'analgons'; images, signs, symbols. These bodies are transported out of themselves and emptied out, as it were, via the eyes; every kind of appeal, incitement and seduction is mobilised to tempt them with doubles of themselves in prettified, smiling and happy poses; this campaign to void them succeeds exactly to the degree that the images proposed correspond to the 'needs' that those same images have helped fashion. So it is that a massive influx of information, of messages, runs head into an inverse flow constituted by the evacuation from the innermost body of all life and desire. Even cars may fulfil the function of analgons, for they are at once extensions of the body and mobile homes, so to speak, fully equipped to receive these wandering bodies. (Lefebvre 1991b, p. 99)

Lefebvre concentrates on the visual nature of representational space which becomes saturated as the subject's eyes consume the 'analgons' which 'void' the subject of the occupancy of their own experience. For Lefebvre, even the 'overlaying' of physical space by the imagination merely constitutes an additional form of superimposed or structurally determined meaning. Adorno's analysis of auditory experience, in which structural imperatives take precedence in the constitution of an 'imaginary', appears to be similar to Lefebvre's. This, potential weakness in their work needs to be addressed in order to gain a more dynamic understanding of personal-stereo use. I argue, somewhat generously perhaps, that their understanding of the colonization of experience that manifests itself in aspects of their work goes against the grain of their own theoretical frameworks in which there can be no mimetic, one-to-one relationship between subject and object, as this would reflect a collapse of the dialectical nature of experience. This drift into determinism I see as a consequence of insufficient attention to empirical study. This is particularly true of Adorno who has an incipient theory of oppositional experience contained in fragmentary form throughout his work to which he nevertheless pays very little attention.

Adorno is, however, aware of the way in which mechanically reproduced sound transforms areas of representational space previously untouched:

> Loudspeaker's installed in the smallest night clubs to amplify the sound until it becomes literally unbearable: everything is to sound like the radio. (Adorno 1991, p. 58)

Adorno's understanding of the relational qualities of the auditory within representational space is useful to our understanding of personal-stereo use, which takes place within a reconstituted and 'privatized' representational space that has even greater immediacy for users than described by Adorno in the 1930s. Adorno makes the point that the club and the radio appear similar, with the club becoming 'like' the radio. Spatial specificity is overlain by an alternative presence and identity in which the present becomes consumed by the 'far away'. Likewise in the following account the isolated space inhabited by the individual disappears:

> Even in the cafe, where one wants to roll up into a ball like a porcupine and become aware on one's insignificance, an imposing loudspeaker effaces every trace of private existence. The announcements it blares forth dominate the space of the concert intermissions, and the waiters (who are listening to it themselves) indignantly refuse the unreasonable request to get rid of this gramophone mimicry. (Kracauer 1995, p. 333)

Kracauer notes that the general desire for distraction becomes more pressing than the general need for silence within urban experience. Technology is perceived as metamorphosing the urban street. For Kracauer this creates a subjective dreamworld, or more accurately a dream form of perception:

> In the evening one saunters through the streets, replete with an unful-
> fillment from which a fullness could sprout. Illuminated words glide by
> on the the rooftops, and already one is banished from one's own
> emptiness into the alien advertisement. One's body takes root in the
> asphalt, and, together with the enlightening revelations of the illumin-
> ations, one's spirit – which is no longer one's own – roams ceaselessly
> out into the night. If only it were allowed to disappear! But, like Pegasus
> prancing on a carousel, this spirit must run in circles and may never tire
> of praising to high heaven the glory of a liqueur and the merits of the
> best five cent cigarette. Some sort of magic spurs that spirit relentlessly
> amid the thousand electric light bulbs, out of which it constitutes and
> reconstitutes itself into glittering sentences. (Kracauer 1995, p. 332)

The process of aestheticization becomes a constituent part of the
urban everyday in a technologized representational space. For Kracauer,
like Lefebvre, this aestheticization constitutes the relational orientation
of the 'subject' and is seen as constituting the 'objective' world that is
absorbed into subjective intentionality. In Adorno's account, in which
'the imposing loudspeaker effaces every trace of private existence', the
subject appears to be engulfed. In contrast to this, Kracauer's subject
who 'is banished from [his] own emptiness into the alien advertise-
ment', might be construed more sympathetically as engaging in an
active process of mimesis in which space becomes a microcosm for the
fantasies or intentions of the experiencing subject. Unfortunately,
Kracauer, like Lefebvre, appears to be locked into the familiar either/or
nature of technological possession in which human agency is framed
within a simplified formula of spatial determination. Kracauer's work,
however, does blur the distinctions between subject and object in a
manner that prefigures the postmodern themes of simulation, hyper-
reality and implosion (Baudrillard 1993). However, Critical Theory's
prognosis of this phenomena, as does my own, differs from that of
later writers in seeing the possible regressive moment in transformed
modes of recognition both individually and socially. Increasingly for
Critical Theorists the technologically produced products of the culture
industry, in all of its forms, become a substitute for the subject's sense
of the social, community or sense of place. This, for Adorno, produces
consumers who become increasingly 'addicted' to using those products
which act as a substitute for the above. Central to this is a transformed
notion of relational experience:

> Addicted conduct generally has a social component: it is one possible
> reaction to the atomisation which, as sociologists have noticed, parallels

the compression of the social network. The addict manages to cope with the situation of social pressure, as well as that of his loneliness, by dressing it up, so to speak, as a reality of his own being; he turns to the formula 'Leave me alone!' into something like an illusory private realm, where he thinks he can be himself. (Adorno 1976a, p. 15)

Music increasingly fills the gap left by the absence of any meaningful sense of the experienced social. Technology is perceived as paradoxically enhancing and increasingly constituting that impoverishment which, for Adorno, contributes to the dependency of the user/listener. Music as such becomes a substitute for community, warmth and social contact. In this isolated world of the listener a need arises to substitute or replace their sense of insecurity with the products of the culture industry, leading to new forms of dependency. Adorno thus brings out what might be considered to be the negative moment in technology and experience. The resulting shift in social spacing, both physical and conceptual implodes subjective experience whereby the lifeworld of the subject becomes a manifestation of mimetic fantasies and unfulfilled desires engendered by the foreclosing of the social from the subject. However it is specifically in the recognition of the 'unfulfilled' articulated through the auditory in Adorno's account that a potentially active formation of agency and intentionality can be found.

Utopian Moments in Repressive Contexts

As always, the thought of utopia is possible only when it finds fragmentary points of references in the here and now. Thus Bloch derives utopia from the 'traces' he finds in the unassuming, irrelevant, and apocryphal, and Adorno follows his lead. (Huhn and Zuidervaart 1997, p. 126)

I have located personal-stereo use dialectically in the present work whereby the relationship between subject and object is perceived in terms of 'non-identity'. As such meaning should not merely be read off from structure but rather should be seen as existing within forms of dialectical tension between 'subject' and 'object'. Given this, an empirical concern with the subjective 'moment' of experience is essential for the development of any critical category of experience. The work of Critical Theorists in the field of urban experience has often been read non-dialectically taking the 'one dimensionality' thesis

(Marcuse 1972b) at face value. In this context social action is reckoned to be totally determined by an all embracing social structure. This is a literal misreading of their work which rather questioned the constitution of the 'subject' within a transformed site and horizon of experience in order to analyse the ideological assumptions and contradictions lying behind the reified use of concepts such as subjective autonomy and so on.

Contemporary cultural accounts of experience frequently use the term as if it were self explanatory, whereas Critical Theorists, following Simmel, reflected on the constitution of differing states of experience whereby forms of integrated experience (*Erfahrung*) were perceived as being progressively displaced by forms of fragmentary experience (*Erlebnis*). My analysis of personal-stereo use investigates the potential dialectic existing between forms of *Erfahrung* within structural conditions of *Erlebnis* in the everyday practices of users. This is demonstrated in user strategies of managing time and experience whereby they construct sites of narrative order in precisely those parts and places of the day that threaten experiential fragmentation. In doing so I question the dualism implicit in notions of active and passive forms of experience so frequently drawn upon to explain everyday behaviour. I have identified potentially utopian moments of resistance in the everyday life of personal-stereo users through their management of space, place and time. Critical Theorists referred to these utopian moments as 'wish landscapes' which were themselves patterned into culture but not strictly identical to it. Adorno referred to this process as one of 'exact fantasy' (Adorno 1977; Nicholson 1997) referring to the changes that the subject can confer onto the object as a potential source of control. The way in which subjects resist colonization, whilst being an important theoretical presence in Critical Theory, remained empirically unexplored and undeveloped. Hence a random reading of Adorno might well indicate the eclipse of intentionality in his understanding of the subject. In order to develop the potentially emancipatory moments of technologically mediated experience I have given far more prominence to the ethnographic details of user strategies which I understand as being intentional in character.

Benjamin, Bloch and Adorno have all pointed to forms of 'compensatory metaphysics' within everyday experience that function as a form of subjective utopian impulse. Whilst Adorno tended to restrict the workings of these concepts to artistic and creative work, I have operationalized them within the realm of the everyday. As such I analyse personal-stereo use in terms of the ways in which users give personal significance to the products of the culture industry. By incorporating an understanding and analysis of the workings of 'compensatory metaphysics' within everyday experience I am able to analyse personal-stereo use in a way that incorporates both an active and utopian, if not unproblematic, dimension in users' experiences.

> The phrase, the world wants to be deceived, has become truer than had ever been intended. People are not only, as the saying goes, falling for the swindle; if it guarantees them even the most fleeting gratification they desire a deception which is nonetheless transparent to them. They force their eyes shut and voice approval, in a kind of self loathing, for what is meted out to them, knowing fully the purpose for which it is manufactured. Without admitting it they sense that their lives would be completely intolerable as soon as they no longer clung to the satisfactions which are none at all. (Adorno 1991, p. 89)

Consumption as such becomes the ambivalent 'refuge for a better state'. (Adorno 1991, p. 45) The objects of consumer culture, especially auditory ones, recreate new forms of relational experience infused with utopian moments of fusion for the subject:

> Socially the hits either channel emotions – thus recognising them – or vicariously fulfil the longing for emotions . . . appearance substitutes for what the listeners are really being denied . . . In an imaginary but psychologically emotion laden domain, the listener who remembers a hit song will turn into the song's ideal subject, into the person for whom the song ideally speaks. At the same time, as one of many who identity with that fictitious subject, he will feel his isolation ease as he himself feels integrated into the community of 'fans'. In whistling such a song he bows to a ritual of socialisation, although beyond this unarticulated subjective stirring of the moment of his isolation continues unchanged. (Adorno 1976a, p. 27)

Adorno's work on technology and experience, importantly for my purposes, focuses upon the acoustic nature of experience and the specific manner in which it connects subject to object. As such it focuses upon the integrative functions specific to auratic experience whereby integration or assimilation becomes a transcendent 'moment' in which the everyday is transformed through the medium of sound. This also provides the 'subjective' moment in Adorno's analysis of the experience of music. Any auditory theory of everyday life needs to confront Critical

Theory's account of the technologization of urban everyday life in order to proceed.

Notes

1. Benjamin positively described the eclipse of aura as being located precisely in the reproducability of artworks, thus taking the work outside of its context in place and time:

> Technical reproduction can put a copy of the original into situations which would be out of reach for the original itself. Above all, it enables the original to meet the beholder half way, be it in the form of a photograph or a phonograph record. The cathedral leaves its locale to be received in the studio of a lover of art; the choral production in an auditorium or in the open air, resounds in the drawing room. (Benjamin 1973b p. 215)

However I suggest that experience is now re-auratized precisely through forms of mechanical reproduction. Notions of the 'original' are themselves historically mediated. The reproduction is the real for contemporary subjects. Often there is no 'real'. Phenomenologically, personal-stereo users experience daily life as potentially auratic. This has something to do with the spatial immediateness of the auditory medium in which subjects can 'get hold' of the experience:

> The desire of contemporary masses to bring things 'closer' spatially and humanely, which is just as ardent as their bent towards overcoming the uniqueness of every reality by accepting its reproduction. Everyday the urge grows stronger to get hold of an object at very close range by way of its likeness, its reproduction. (Benjamin 1973b, p. 217)

2. Howard Caygill (1998) has pointed to the significance of 'monumentalization' in Benjamin's work. Monumentalization is a term used to describe the denial of the contingent and the passage of time. Benjamin originally used it to discuss the relation of the subject to the object in fascist Germany. Through Nazi propaganda, subjects would monumentalize the state and the 'timeless' icons of its identity. As Caygill observes:

> The same photographic technology that in the hands of Atget could open itself to contingency was also capable of re-creating aura and fixing the image

of a monumental present. Instead of transforming experience by making it contingent and open to future interpretation, technology may well serve to monumentalize it. (Caygill 1998, p. 95)

I am rather more interested in highlighting the way in which personal-stereo users tend to monumentalize their experience through the auditory. Monumentalization becomes an everyday experiential strategy. This does not mean that it has similar political import to Benjamin's discussion of it. The monumentalization is of the subject's own experience yet constructed through the personalization of music.

3. As such, the findings of Critical Theorists need not be in contradiction of subcultural studies and audience-research work carried out in the tradition of Morley (1992) and others.

Visual Theories of City Life and Personal-Stereo Use

A suspicion is circulating: our culture until now has been primarily determined by vision, is in the process of becoming an auditative culture.

W. Welsch, *Undoing Aesthetics*

Having outlined an auditory and dialectical account of urban experience in the previous chapter it might appear that I am discounting notions of visuality completely. Nothing could be further from the truth. Indeed I have devoted two chapters of the phenomenology of personal-stereo use to forms of auditory looking. The point I wish to make is that a reliance upon visual epistemologies to explain auditory forms of experience leads to systematic errors of interpretation. Whilst visually based explanations of urban behaviour have considerable explanatory power, my own study highlights the way in which this visual primacy fails to explain the relational nature of auditory experience sufficiently. However, to discount visual accounts completely would be to commit the same error I attribute to visually based theories of urban experience. The phenomenology of personal-stereo use does demonstrate the partial relevance of visual explanations together with the need to re-evaluate them. Visually based explanations are loosely drawn under three 'interwoven' processes: that of a retreating (Simmel 1997a), an aestheticizing (Bauman 1993; Jenks 1995; Tester 1994) and an indifferent subjectivity (Sennett 1990, 1994).

Urban Subjects as Retreating Subjects: The Work of Simmel

Motifs of urban escape have increasingly becomes the paradigm within which an understanding of the management of urban space is situated.

These explanations derive largely from Simmel's work on the city. Simmel focuses upon vision as a window on the soul which is in need of protection from an urban visual overload. Within this scenario the subject becomes vulnerable to the encroaching 'gaze' of others within a swiftly moving urban environment which the eye fails to incorporate successfully and coherently. In presenting his analysis Simmel moves from an analysis of the senses to an understanding of the interpersonal:

> The interpersonal relationships of people in big cities are characterised by a markedly greater emphasis on the use of the eyes than that of the ears. This can be attributed to the institution of public conveyances. Before buses, railroads and trains became fully established during the nineteenth century, people were never in a position to have to stare at one another for minutes or even hours on end without exchanging a word. (Simmel in Benjamin 1973, p. 151)

Simmel, unlike most other urbanists, was attentive to the relationship and significance of seeing and hearing within urban culture. He also incorporated technology, albeit limited to modes of transport, as a defining feature of the changing urban world of city dwellers, resulting in the transformation of urban forms of spatiality that constitutes, in turn, the context of physical and sensory proximity in people's interpersonal realm. Simmel's description of the urban citizen is of a subjectivity in retreat, fleeing from an overload of sensory stimulation which threatens them. A fragile subjective order is created by strategies of exclusion in which the urban environment is managed through the taking up of a 'blasé attitude.

> (Urban conditions require) an inner barrier between people, a barrier, however, that is indispensable for the modern form of life. For the jostling crowdedness and the motley disorder of metropolitan communication would simply be unbearable without such psychological distance. Since contemporary urban culture, with its commercial, professional and social intercourse, forces us to be physically close to an enormous number of people, sensitive and nervous people would sink completely into despair if the objectification of social relationships did not bring with it an inner boundary and reserve. (Simmel 1997a, p. 178)

The blasé attitude constituted a defence against the perceived threat of city life in which engulfment was conceived of as both physical and psychical. Williamson understands personal-stereo use within this explanatory framework:

> The Walkman is primarily a way of escaping from a shared experience or environment. It produces a privatized sound, in the public domain, a weapon of the individual against the communal. It attempts to negate chance ... the walk-person is buffered against the unexpected – an apparent triumph of individual control over social spontaneity. (Williamson 1990, p. 209)

The belief that urban subjects are subjects in retreat has become a core explanatory framework of everyday urban behaviour. Alternatively retreat is perceived as a strategy of coping with an urban environment experienced as being inhabited by 'strangers' and hence dangerous. This is typical of visual explanations of urban behaviour that locate motivation completely in terms of supposed responses to the environment.

> The techniques of mismeeting and civil inattention are the tools of social/cognitive spacing. They produce the Other primarily as the stranger which best melts into the meaningless physical space: the unavoidable nuisance one would prefer to live without, yet one cannot. Under the circumstances, the sole knowledge one seeks of the strangers is how to keep them in their status as strangers. (Bauman 1993, p. 168)

This bleak understanding of urban spaces is often overgeneralized however. Urban subjects are just as likely to experience the city as places of familiarity, of play or of boredom. Yet even such an acute observer of urban life as Goffman describes the city in terms of the precariousness of habitation:

> The vulnerability of public life is what we're coming more and more to see. Certainly in the great public forums of our society, the downtown areas of our cities, can come to be uneasy places. Militantly sustained antagonisms between diffusely intermingled major population segments – young and old, male and female, white and black, impoverished and well off – can cause those in public gatherings to distrust (and to fear they are distrusted by) the person standing next to them. The forms of civil inattention of persons circumspectly treating one another with polite and glancing concern while each goes about his separate business, may be maintained, but behind these normal appearances individuals can

come to be at the ready, poised to flee or to fight back if necessary and in place of unconcern there can be alarm – until, that is, the streets are redefined as naturally precarious places, and a high level of risk becomes routine. (Goffman 1971, p. 386)

Whilst Simmel's categories of explanation are not under dispute I do question their general applicability to everyday urban experience. It becomes far too easy to fall back on explanatory categories developed at the turn of the century in order to produce generalized explanations of contemporary urban experience. My own analysis has demonstrated that notions of a retreating subjectivity are one structural response to the habitation of urban spaces. Equally I have demonstrated that users sometimes use personal stereos to shield themselves from the encroachment of potentially unwanted attention from others. However, the notion of retreating subjectivity still requires to be understood auditorily in order to fully understand the actual relational strategies of personal-stereo users in their everyday experience. My own analysis indicates that personal-stereo users are equally motivated by a range of alternative management imperatives ranging from solipsistic reverie to strategies of asymmetric control which remain 'unseen' in visually based explanations of everyday behaviour.

Aestheticizing the Street: Goodbye to the Flâneur

The aesthetic nature of everyday experience has become a dominant motif in accounts of urban life. These writings, often deriving from the work of Benjamin, have now incorporated a more postmodern slant in which the aesthetic becomes a liberatory space of urban experience within which personal-stereo use is but one example. Personal-stereo users are, as I have noted, skilled strategists of auditory looking. The act of 'looking' to manufactured sound is inscribed in the behaviour of any urban citizen who has grown up with television, film and video and this is reinforced as they move around urban spaces with its canned music filling public spaces. An integral part of the visuality of these mediums is the musical soundtrack that accompanies them, supplementing the narrative and giving an emotionally heightened expression to the image. The pervasiveness of the socializing function of these mediums has been an increasingly important concern of social research which has, however, often led to generalized accounts of the influence of these mediums in the construction of subjectivity and experience:

Reality as it was visually experienced, became a staged social production. Real, everyday experiences came to be judged against their staged, cinematic, video counterpart. The metaphor of the dramaturgical society, or 'life as theatre' ceased to be just a metaphor. It became an interactional reality. (Denzin 1995, p. 34)

We live in a video, cinematic age, where the cinematic apparatus intervenes between the material world and everyday, lived experience. (Denzin 1995, p. 200)

Denzin claims that the aesthetics of communication mediums are transposed into all areas of social life in the form of a Baudrillardian simulation where differential meanings collapse. We thus live in a social world of simulation. Life as theatre becomes an everyday interactional reality from this viewpoint. Urban experience was first described in these terms in the situationist writings of Debord in the 1960s. However Denzin's account lacks the critical edge of Debord's:

In societies where modern conditions prevail, all of life presents itself as an immense accumulation of spectacles. Everything that was directly lived has moved away into representation. (Debord 1977, p. 5)

For Debord, the experiencing subject is locked into a subjectification of experience by viewing the interactional no longer as interactional but as representational. Debord's account of social experience is 'solipsistic' and facets of personal-stereo use do indeed replicate this point. Denzin merely collapses the spectacle into a form of unspecified interactional reality whereas it is precisely the status and nature of any such 'interactional reality' that should be questioned. Debord in contrast sees this process as an alienating one:

The world of consumption is in reality the world of mutual specularisation of everyone, the world of everyone's separation, estrangement and nonparticipation . . . the spectacle is the dominant mode through which people relate to one another. It is only through the spectacle that people acquire a [falsified] knowledge of certain general aspects of social life . . . It answers perfectly the needs of a reified and alienated culture. (Debord 1977, p. 55)

Alternatively writers focus more modestly and specifically and on the nature and genesis of the 'gaze' in urban space:

The virtual gaze is not a direct perception but a received perception mediated through representation. I introduce this compound term in order to describe a gaze that travels in an imaginary elsewhere. The mobilised gaze has a history, which begins well before the cinema and is rooted in other cultural activities that involve walking and travel. . . The gradual shift into post modernity is marked, I argue, by the increased centrality of the mobilised gaze as a fundamental feature of everyday life. (Friedberg 1993, pp. 2–4)

Whilst Freidberg's attempts to historicize the 'virtual gaze' by seeing it as an extension of traditional modes of experiencing, she does so by continuing to tie it to the nineteenth-century notion of 'flânerie':

Flânerie will serve as an exemplary device to trace changes in represent-ation and the aesthetic of experience in the nineteenth century. As a social and textual construct for mobile visuality, flânerie can be histor-ically situated as an urban phenomenon linked in gradual but direct ways, the new aesthetic of reception found in 'moviegoing' . . . The gradual shift into post modernity is marked, I argue, by an increased centrality of the mobilised gaze as a fundamental feature of everyday life. (Friedberg 1993, pp. 3–4)

Whilst visits to diorama's, looking at postcards or going to the cinema quite rightly might be perceived as historical antecedents to todays 'mobilized gazing', she nevertheless fails to address the specificity of contemporary 'gazing', preferring instead to coin the term 'imaginary flânerie' to describe urban experiencing. 'Literary' reconstructions of urban behaviour invariably fall back onto traditional conceptual formulations to explain contemporary forms of behaviour. Not surpris-ingly they resurrect inappropriate concepts such as *flânerie* to explain contemporary behaviour. It is my contention that notions of *flânerie* are not useful either in explaining general forms of urban behaviour and more specifically are inappropriate as a tool for understanding personal-stereo use. Furthermore, the use of 'flânerie' as an analytical concept within cultural and urban study masks an unreflective under-standing of the role of urban aesthicization in everyday life.

Flânerie is virtually the only concept that urban and cultural theorists take from the early work of the Frankfurt School. In the work of Benjamin, flânerie represents the aesthetic reappropriation of exper-ience and is largely a visual experience in which the subjects observe the 'crowd' but do not see themselves as a part of it. As such, the urban becomes a reflection of the desire of the urban dweller. Accounts of urban experience that incorporate Benjamin's work on the 'flâneur' in support of their position ignore Benjamin's own dismissal of the concept as an obsolete category in the twentieth-century city together with his negative evaluation of *flânerie*. For Benjamin, the *flâneur* represented the increasing alienation and commodification of urban experience:

> [The flâneur has the 'allorgorist's gaze'] of an alienated man. It is the gaze of the flâneur, whose way of living still bestowed a conciliatory gleam over the growing destitution of man in the great city. The flâneur still stood at the margin, of the great city as of the bourgeois class. Neither of them had yet overwhelmed him. In neither of them was he at home. He sought his asylum in the crowd ... The crowd was the veil from behind which the familiar city as phantasmagoria beckoned to the flâneur. In it, the city was now landscape, now a room ... For the private individual the private environment represents the universe. In it he gathers remote places and the past. His drawing room is a box in the world theatre ... the gaze of the allegorist that falls on the city is estranged. It is the gaze of the flâneur, whose mode of life still surrounds the approaching desolation of city life with a propitiatory luster ... The crowd is the veil through which the familiar city lures the flâneur like a phantasmagoria. In it the city is now a landscape, now a room. Both, then, constitute the department store that puts even flânerie to use for commodity circulation. The department store is the flâneur's last practical joke. (Benjamin 1986, p. 155–6)

The critical and historical contextualization of the flâneur provided by Benjamin is largely ignored in contemporary accounts which prefer to situate the flâneur within a postmodern context of aesthetic freedom. Benjamin's flâneurs observed and kept a distance from the 'crowd' wishing both to merge with it and transcend it. This alienating and objectifying gaze was a product of the flâneur not being at one with the crowd, hence their literary pedigree deriving from the thoughts of Baudelaire. Flânerie, however, became a dominant motif in writings on personal-stereo use together with many other accounts of urban experience. The work of Hosokawa (1984) and Chambers (1994), for example, situate personal-stereo use within forms of urban social contestation and de-centred experience drawing theoretically upon the work of De Certeau (1988) and Deleuze and Guattari (1987). In these accounts users become 'nomadic rebels' or 'flâneurs' experientially remaking their urban experience aesthetically as de-centred subjects. If indeed flâneurs respond to and record the phenomena of the street then it is apparent that personal-stereo users are not flâneurs in the accepted sense of the word. In their solipsistic aesthetic recreation of experience the empirical facticity of the street is more often than not ignored or discounted, as has already been noted.

Despite Benjamin's own critique and with little empirical justification, flânerie has become the paradigmatic account of urban looking and experience. Jenks (1995) considers both the empirical 'facticity' of the 'flâneur' and its analytical value as a concept that contributes to our understanding of contemporary urban experience:

> I seek to reconstitute the analytical force of the flâneur. The flâneur is the metaphoric figure originally brought into being by Baudelaire, as the SPECTATOR and DEPICTER of modern life, most specifically in relation to contemporary art and sights of the city. The flâneur moves through space and among the people with a viscosity that both enables and privileges vision . . . The flâneur, though grounded in everyday life, is an analytical form, a narrative device, an attitude towards knowledge and its social context. It is an image of movement through the social space of modernity . . . The flâneur is a multilayered palimpsest that enables us to 'move' from real products of modernity, like commodif-ication and leisured patriarchy, through the practical organisation of space and its negotiation by inhabitants of a city, to a critical appreciation of the state of modernity and its erosion into the post-, and to a reflexive understanding of the function, and purpose, of realist as opposed to hermeneutic epistemologies in the appreciation of those previous formations. (Jenks 1995, pp. 146–9)

This de-historizing of Benjamin is typical of accounts of urban behaviour that come from the library rather than the street. In this celebration of *flânerie* most writers, Debord excepted, appear to be immune to the idea that there might be something problematic with the aesthetic-ization of everyday life that would require critical investigation:

> Social/cognitive spacing has created distances which aesthetic spacing can transgress only playfully, only in the imagination, only incon-sequentially. The strangers who appear in the flâneur's play is but the sight of the stranger. (Bauman 1994, p. 153)

The aesthetic mode of urban appropriation is thus described as both harmless and subjectively empowering. I have demonstrated that personal-stereo users are indeed empowered yet this tells us very little about the qualitative or relational qualities of these strategies. Should we understand them as liberatory, merely harmless or as representing the alienating, objectifying tendencies of our culture in which modes of difference are habitually unrecognized?

The aestheticization of experience is one structural possibility of personal-stereo use. The power to successfully aestheticize lies in the technological artifact. Personal-stereo users, it will be remembered, found it difficult to conjure up the appropriate imagery without sound. I would go further than this and claim that habitual modes of contemporary aestheticization are inconceivable without their technological construction. Aesthetic empowerment is technologically mediated and dependent. Equally the status of aesthetic control is problematic, at least in terms of personal-stereo use. Personal-stereo users, in controlling their experience, appear to negate difference in colonizing space and place. They, unlike *flâneurs*, are not concerned with aesthetically drawing in the urban world but rather with solipsistically transcending it. The nature of and implications of aesthetic control in interpersonal urban spaces is an issue I take up in detail in Chapter Twelve where rather than focusing upon Benjamin's work on *flânerie* I discuss aestheticization in relation to his work on technology and the senses.

Indifferent Cities

One dominant motif displayed by personal-stereo users is one of indifference to the urban environment. Richard Sennett, who has provided an impressive analysis of the historical nature and trajectory of urban experience focuses precisely upon an understanding of the nature of indifference. He, rather like Simmel and Benjamin before him, takes a favoured city as the basis of his analysis: New York, in which the urban dweller withdraws all but visually from the city. This orientation is fostered and continued through the creation and inscription of urban spaces that reflect the values of individualism and Protestantism. Central to Sennett's analysis, like Simmel before him, is the reorganization of sensory experience within the urban. However, Sennett's primary distinction is between the senses of touch and sight in which a progressive deadening of the senses of touch is replaced by vision as the creator of subjective order. He states that:

> In the course of the development of modern, urban individualism, the individual fell silent in the city. The street, the cafe, the department store,

the railroad, bus and underground became places of gaze rather than scenes of discourse. The verbal connections between strangers in the modern city are difficult to sustain, the impulses of sympathy which individuals may feel in the city looking at the scene around become in turn momentary – a second of response looking at snapshots of life . . . ours is a purely visual agora. (Sennett 1994, p. 358)

The mundanity of the geography of the city is both neutral and repelling. Bauman, in support of this, claims that:

For every resident of the modern world, social space is spattered over a vast sea of meaninglessness in the form of numerous larger and smaller blots of knowledge: oases of meaning and relevance amidst a featureless desert. Much of daily experience is spent travelling through semiotically empty spaces – moving physically from one island to another... To preserve their respective identities measures need to be taken – to keep strangers confined to their places. (Bauman 1993, p. 158)

Sennett and Bauman, like Simmel, restrict technology to the role it plays in transportation of urban citizens. The prioritizing of vision goes hand in hand with a perceived pacification of the body, as in the following description of driving through the city.

The traveller experiences the world in narcotic terms; the body moves passively, desensitised in space, to destinations set in a fragmented and discontinuous urban geography . . . Through the sense of touch we risk feeling something or someone as alien. Our technology permits us to avoid that risk. (Sennett 1990, p. 18)

Within this passivized space the urban subject is portrayed as experiencing the city with minimal risk. Sennett is alluding to Simmel's portrayal of the city as being full of 'strangers' towards which Sennett's subject is supremely indifferent. This indifference is located not necessarily in a blasé attitude created by sensory overload but from the subjects cultural indifference. The urbanite has no real interest in the 'other' but merely wishes to be left alone to take in the scene 'narcotically':

Individual bodies moving through urban space gradually became detached from the space in which they moved, and from the people the space contained. As space became devalued through motion, individuals gradually lost a sense of sharing a fate with others . . . individuals create something like ghettos in their own bodily experience. (Sennett 1994, p. 366)

The powerful metaphor of the 'ghetto' refers to a protected zone of mobile presence that the urban dweller is said to desire in the face of diversity. Sennett's subjects exist on similarity and are merely voyeurs of urban diversity. Their 'looks' become one of spectatorial indifference. Silencing is not a product of psychology but of social condition. The geography of the city reflects a set of social values that reproduce cities as 'empty spaces' within which privatized individuals willingly move. In this withdrawal the individual is perceived as being 'free'. This social production of isolation is related to the belief that:

one's surroundings [do not] have any meaning save as a means towards the end of one's own motion . . . isolation in the midst of public visibility. A person feels he must protect himself from the surveillance of others in the public realm by social isolation. (Sennett 1994, p. 15)

This self-imposed isolation has certain social antecedents in bourgeois notions of distance and civility enabling the urban dweller to maintain a sense of privacy wherein public life becomes tolerable. Sennett believes that with this heightened sense of subjective value the civility of the bourgeois past has crumbled. This theme is taken up in the present work by drawing upon Adorno's and Honneth's analyses of the 'moral' spacings of urban behaviour. Sennett attributes this 'crumbling' as being due both to the subjectivization of experience and to the subsequent stripping away of visually interesting urban spaces which creates what Sennett refers to as, a silent wilderness which in turn legitimates this withdrawal:

The defence against being read by others was to stop feeling – one's behaviour in public was altered in its fundamental terms. Silence in public became the only way one could experience public life, without being overwhelmed . . . There grew up a notion that strangers had no right to speak to one another, that each man possessed as a public right an invisible shield, a right to be left alone. Public behaviour was a matter of observation, of passive participation, of a certain kind of voyeurism . . . Knowledge was no longer to be produced by social intercourse . . . isolation in the midst of visibility to others was a logical consequence of insisting on one's right to be mute when one ventured in this chaotic yet still magnetic realm. (Sennett 1994, p. 27)

The public realm is perceived to be both magnetic and repulsing at the same time. Those sentiments encouraging silence and privacy in the city suggests an explanation as to the ease with which new forms of technology, such as personal stereos, that further these impulses have been developed and taken up with such enthusiasm and success in urban culture. Though Sennett does not develop this theme it seems likely that new developments in the privatization of experience together with a furthering of asymmetrical social encounters are enshrined in these new technological artifacts as indeed are notions of withdrawal. However, Sennett overlooks important alternative elements in the constitution of withdrawal that might aid an adequate explanation of personal-stereo use. This lies in a reformulation of the constitution of relational experience mediated through technology. Personal-stereo users move in public isolation but are not alone in their mediated flights of the imagination. Users are never 'alone' as theirs is a more intimate yet more 'isolated' form of company.

In this chapter I have analysed the potential contribution that visually based epistemologies of urban experience might have in relation to personal-stereo use. They all, however, fail to address the specificity of the auditory nature of experience. Neither do they sufficiently address the increasingly technologically mediated nature of everyday experience, a concern addressed in the following chapter.

Technology and the Management of Everyday Life

Since phenomenologically, everydayness is constituted as a living, extended or durational present, in principle incomplete, it cannot be structured by repetition alone. Rather, it is the place where the riddle of recurrence, intercepts the theory of becoming.

P. Osborne, *The Politics of Time*

In a sense all experience for Benjamin is technological, since the term technology designates the artificial organisation of perception; as such, experience changes with the development of technology . . . he proposed a notion of technology as a medium of organisation which patterned experience while being reciprocally subject to change in the face of experience.

H. Caygill, *Walter Benjamin*

The everyday experience of personal-stereo users is imbued with a range of strategies aimed at managing increasing portions of their daily life. I have described these strategies as being habitually asymmetrical whether it be in strategies of looking, interpersonal engagement or attending to the urban spaces passed through. Personal-stereo users also demonstrate an acute awareness of the fragility and potential oppressiveness of the everyday and manage this perceived contingency through the use of their personal stereo. This technologized form of management has not arisen in a social and cultural vacuum. Rather, personal-stereo use can be located within an historical and cultural trajectory in which traditional forms of face-to-face communication

147

increasingly compete with technologically simulated forms of experience that are perceived of as being more attractive, predicable and secure to users. The phenomenology of personal-stereo use has illustrated the complex manner in which users routinely enact patterns of asymmetrical interpersonal contact within the everyday. Users have been described as being continually accompanied by the mediated sounds of their personal stereos whereby they manage their relations in public through their own personalized and manufactured auditory.

The generation of experience through technology and the cultural predispositions or cultural imperatives that lie behind it poses a question concerning the relation between technological experience and unmediated forms of direct experience within urban spaces. This constitutes the moral spacing of urban culture which has been a common concern of writers from a wide variety of theoretical perspectives from Simmel to Honneth. However, few have located explanations concerning this moral spacing of behaviour in the interface between technology, cultural values and experience as I do in the present study.

In order to fully understand this process it is necessary to situate personal-stereo use critically within the use of other forms of communication technologies. Previous work in this field has often discounted the relational consequences attached to the use of such technologies. In the following pages I focus upon the use and role of communication technologies in the generation of habitual forms of managing everyday life, in order to situate personal-stereo use within the framework of other communication technologies.

Personal Stereos, Communication Technologies and Everyday Life: A Critical Evaluation

Technologically mediated and constructed behaviour is, as the analysis of personal-stereo use indicates, heightened behaviour. Critical Theorists were aware of this phenomenon as early as the 1930s. Benjamin described the camera as acting as a form of 'optical unconscious' whilst Adorno was acutely aware of the reconstitution of presence engendered through music reception together with the manipulative and suggestive role that music played within film (Adorno and Eisler 1994). Technology thus became important in terms of its role in reconfiguring the site and constitution of experience.

The prioritizing of individual experience and desire through forms of communication technology is embedded in a variety of daily social practices. Within the home it is signified by the positioning of televisions in bedrooms, along with video and hi-fi equipment (Silverstone and Hirsch 1992). In public, it is represented by personal stereos, car radios and increasingly, through the use of mobile phones. Many personal-stereo users describe patterns of childhood use in the home or in the family car, listening whilst parents were otherwise engaged. Personal-stereo use enabled users to reinscribe their own desires within those situations holding no interest to them. The analysis of personal-stereo use outlined in earlier chapters appears to indicate that the social network within which people move on an everyday basis has undergone a recent transformation. Users appear to be increasingly retreating from direct interactive forms of behaviour and increasingly identifying with a manufactured sense of 'we-ness' embodied in representational space construed as 'music space'. As such personal-stereo use exemplifies an implicit set of attitudes to the social which are instrumentalist and asymmetrical.[1] Personal-stereo use represents a way of 'being in the world' in which technology constitutes an accompaniment to and mediator of the mundane everyday construction of social experience. In order to explain the role of technological artifacts within both the structural realm of culture and the experiential realm of the everyday it is necessary to give due weight to the placing of technology within the everyday. This in no way implies attributing to it a deterministic or monocausal function. For example, it is possible to discuss the structural functions of television without necessarily falling into an image of passive consumers. More interestingly, television use has been historically tied to both the process and furtherance of individualism, privatization and the changing constitution of family life in the West as well as with the transformation of lived family space.[2] Communication processes are thus both mediated and constituted by transformations in the home as well as in public spaces.

The relationship between communication practices and forms of technology have been investigated and speculated upon since the early Payne Fund Studies. However, research has recently tended to concentrate on the domestic placing and context of pieces of communication technology examining their relationship to patterns of domestic use, often stressing the gender or intra-familial aspects of use. One of the main purposes of this type of research has been to rehabilitate the consumer as an autonomous choice maker. The consumer thus becomes sovereign and the research describes the myriad number of ways that consumers exercise their choice in relation to themselves, other family members and friends. The problems involved in this type of research are multiple. The work of Lull, which in many respects is an excellent piece of ethnography, is typical of this type of approach to technology and communication:

> Mass media can be viewed as important and uniquely employed social resources in interpersonal communications systems. They are handy expedients which can be exploited by individuals, coalitions, and family units to serve their personal needs, create practical relationships, and engage the social world. Television and other mass media, rarely mentioned as vital forces in the construction or maintenance of interpersonal relations, can now be seen to play central roles in the methods which families and other social units employ to interact normatively. The interpersonal use one makes of the mass media constitute the construction of a particular subset of actions which find practical applications in the home environment. (Lull 1990, p. 29–30)

Whilst Lull's work on domestic television use gives a useful insight into the context of structural and regulative use within interpersonal domestic settings, his analysis remains largely descriptive and suffers both from the hypostasizing of the category of experience as well as that of technology. It is also typical in its separation of the domestic sphere of the everyday from the social structures within which these practices are situated. This lack of theoretical reflection on the qualitative constitution of social experience results in a neglect of the political, social and historical context within which these practices are situated. The consequences of treating technology and the interpersonal in this way is that there is a tendency to treat all behaviour as functionally given thereby leaving the wider constitution and contexts of choices unexamined. This positivistic circumscribing of social practices produce an implicit assumption that description is explanation. The ideological meaning of behaviour mediated and constructed within a changing technological environment is taken for granted or assumed, whereas I argue that it is precisely this which is of theoretical significance.

Other work has gone some way to addressing some of these limitations. For example, it has been argued that forms of communication technology and the competition over their use represents general cultural values relating to individualism, gender or class. This has led researchers to investigate how communication technologies in the home either reinforce or subvert gender patterns of authority in the home (Silverstone and Hirsch 1992). Another way of productively looking at the relationship between culture, content and the use of a given technology is given by Provenzo, writing in relation to computer games, where he argues that:

Video games such as Nintendo, through a process of incorporation, have the potential to amplify certain values (for example, women as victims; women as individuals who are acted upon rather than initiating action; women as dependent rather than independent). In doing so, the games reflect a larger cultural hegemony that functions on multiple levels. (Provenzo 1991, p. 46)

The cultural predisposition of game content, he argues, tends to exclude girls from the outset. Provenzo does not limit his analysis to merely maintaining that, if the games somehow transcended the gender stereotypes within culture, they could be played equally amongst both sexes. The general ideological predisposition of the playing of the games in terms of the generation and reflection of cultural and social preferences reflected in use becomes a central concern of this type of analysis. Equally Selnow in his analysis of children's use of video games argues that they have certain ramifications concerning their relation to interpersonal behaviour:

Video games rate higher than human companionship – the games were viewed as more exiting and more fun than human companions . . . [through the game medium] they are transported from life's problems by their playing, they experience a sense of personal involvement in the action when they work the controls, and they view video games as not only a source of companionship, but possibly a substitute for it. Heavy users of video games may be 'satisfying' their companionship need with video games rather than with less available [less fun, less exiting] human companions. (Selnow 1984, p. 63–4)

This prioritization of experience is learnt through the activity of playing the games and becomes part of the child's taken-for-granted everyday behaviour. The work of Sherry Turkle also follows this line of investigation in her discussion of communicating through MUDs on the internet:

Virtual communities ranging from MUDs to computer bulletin boards allow people to generate experiences, relationships, identities, and living spaces that only arise through interaction with technology . . . We have learnt to take things at interface value. We are moving toward a culture of simulation in which people are increasingly comfortable with substituting representations of reality for the real. (Turkle 1995, p. 21–3)

At present I only wish to take up Turkle's theme of the transformation of interpersonal experience rather than the transformation of space, or the imaginary spaces which provide the material of communicatory practices. Turkle points to the historical derivation and normalization of modes of communication. She notes a comment made to her by one respondent:

> Who was upset by what she described as the flight of her friends to the internet, 'Now they just want to talk online. It used to be that things weren't so artificial. We used to phone each other every afternoon.' To this young woman, phone calls represented the natural, intimate and immediate. We build our ideas about what is real and what is natural with the cultural means available. (Turkle 1995, p. 237)

Turkle claims that for MUD users the 'real' is necessarily perceived to be not as interesting or as stimulating as the virtual. Whilst this point is hardly novel and exists in several variants within postmodern thought, her concern with the interactive potential of technology reflects key concerns within the present chapter's analysis of contextualizing personal-stereo use. She situates use dialectically by pointing to the consequences of the privatizing tendencies of technology together with the communicative transformation and potential of the same technology. One part of this dialectic in the context of MUDs is the retreat of some users into 'virtual' communities:

> Women and men tell me that the rooms and mazes on MUDs are safer than city streets, virtual sex is safer than sex anywhere, MUD friendships are more intense than real ones, and when things don't work out you can always leave. (Turkle 1995, p. 244)

To understand the use of MUDs it becomes necessary not merely to discuss the structural propensities attached to their use but also to locate their use within the cultural values within which use is situated; the generation of those cultural values and the everyday lifeworld of people patterned and structured by the urban environment within which these practices occur. Personal-stereo use also takes its place within a cultural environment saturated with communication technologies and their products (Baudrillard 1993; Jameson 1991; Poster 1995). The above analysis permits us to connect the use of personal stereos to other forms of domestic communication technologies. Through an imaginative reading of previous literature it is possible to connect habitual forms of use to both existing cultural values and technological design.

Personal stereos, however, radically extend users' abilities to control or manage experience so that many previously immune or excluded realms of the everyday are now included within technological mediation. The present analysis permits us to move out of the domestic environment of the user into the public realm of the street in order to investigate how users' habitual dispositions towards their experience extends into realms of the 'impersonal' made habitable through the use of personal stereos.

Managing Contingency

Throughout this study it has been apparent that personal-stereo use is not explained merely by recourse to the physical presence of urban spaces but is more appropriately understood through solipsistic preoccupations with a fragile narcissism fed through, amongst other things, forms of 'we-ness'. Users, through their efforts to negate the perceived contingency of the everyday that lies in wait for them, create habitual forms of cognitive management based on personal-stereo use that blurs any distinctions that might be made between inner and outer, the public and private areas of everyday life.

The object of regulation for users varies as does its significance among different users. Personal-stereo use produces a successful technological intervention in the implementation of any desired cognitive state for users. Users invariably are not able to successfully emulate this type of management without the use of their personal stereos. Moreover, it appears that users come, through habitual use, to develop an orientation to the regulation of their cognition in public and in private that is largely dependent upon technology. It is instructive to see these patterns of dependency or orientation to the everyday management of experience as being conditioned through the habitual use of other forms of information technology from an early age. Users have learnt to trust other pieces of communication technology in the organization and management of their daily experience although not all are as successful as the use of a personal stereo. Users appear to becomes dependent on the use of personal stereos in order to obtain a certain 'fix', just as a person might become habitually orientated to any number of other artifacts, activities or substances (Provenzo 1991; Turkle 1995).

The mobility of personal stereos enable users to maintain contact with their favourite types of music around which aspects of their own social identity, orientations and interests are formed and constituted.

Other users may pick up a personal stereo later in life in order to ameliorate feelings of boredom whilst commuting or use them in specific sporting activities such as jogging, swimming or skiing. In these situations the user's desire and ability to prioritize their own desires in public is set in place. The use of personal stereos creates a sense of security and comfort in public which is a central component of its use together with its function as a time filler, mood enhancer and motivator.

Many users choose specific music to play on their machines in order to achieve their desired effect. They may have 'personal stereo tapes' containing a personal or narrative attachment, or their tape may include music that has a proven track record of enabling them to face the world more successfully. It is precisely users' chosen connection to the products of the culture industry through both the artifact of the personal stereo and its 'sound' that enables them to prioritize and implement one set of desires and orientations over others. In doing so users attempt to impose order onto both the perceived potential chaos that might exist both in the ordering of their senses and onto the contingency of the everyday that continually confronts them publicly. As such the use of personal stereos reduce both interior and external 'risk'. Silverstone has pointed to a variety of this type of orientation with reference to television use:

> Everyday life, it is argued cannot be sustained without order – an order manifested in our various traditions, rituals, routines and taken for granted activities – in which we, paradoxically, invest so much energy, effort and so many cognitive and emotional resources. In the ordering of daily life we avoid panic, we construct and maintain our identities, we manage our social relationships in time and space, sharing meanings . . . but avoiding for the most part the blank and numbing horror of the threat of chaos. (Silverstone 1994, p. 16)

The rituals surrounding and constituting everyday life through communication technologies give users the expectation and impression of having and subsequently needing much greater management potential over their everyday experience in all of its forms than had previously been imagined. The changing constitution and ordering of time, space and social relationships within domestic environments through communication technologies can be seen to prefigure the development and use of the personal stereos in reconfiguring these relationships in potentially every social or public environment. Personal-stereo use highlights the strategies of extending order into realms of existence otherwise largely immune from technological intervention and construction. There are, however, structural problems attached to these types of strategy. Cohen and Taylor, like Critical Theorists before them, point out the structural and empirical problems of using the 'inner life' as a 'sanctuary' from the object world within which thought and action are situated:

> The problem for those who would rely upon the inner life as a sanctuary from the routines and repetitions of life, as a private site where personal identity might be assiduously cultivated, arises not only from ways in which society regulates and shapes the nature of that inner life, but also from the difficulties in effecting continuity between our imaginings. We experience the external world as bound together by time and space, it spreads before us in an ordered and predictable manner. But often the purely inner life is far more random and inchoate. Sometimes we literally cannot get our fantasies going. We lie back and wait but they will not unroll, our inner eye refuses to travel, remaining myopically fixed upon a single obstinate image. We respond by feeding it with further stimuli, we gaze at pictures, read books, assemble relevant properties. We try to facilitate the appearance and development of our fantasy by constructing a compatible external world. . . By resorting to such activities, we reveal the unsuitability of fantasy as a means for genuinely transforming our lives. (Cohen and Taylor 1976, p. 102)

This account of everyday life was originally written in the mid-1970s and pre- dates personal-stereo use. It is useful in demonstrating the historical variability attached to any such 'escape attempts'. My analysis of personal stereo use demonstrates that the relationship between volition and success in mood management is indeed historically situated and technologically mediated. Contemporary personal-stereo users, do not experience barriers to the successful negotiation and orientation of their experience in the manner described above by Cohen and Taylor.

To the extent that use facilitates a withdrawal from the external world it can also be argued that the desire for centredness through the management of experience is an attempt to maintain a sense of coherence over time. The construction or maintenance of a sense of narrative is inscribed into many user practices. Understood in this manner, use can be interpreted as a strategy aimed at achieving a greater sense of integrated experience (*Erfahrung*) within the perceived daily world of fragmentary experience (*Erlebnis*). Personal-stereo use represents the dual aim of management of the subjective as well as management of the environment within which experience takes place. Users do indeed, following Sennett, tend to make ghettos of their own experience in public. This use of personal stereos can be interpreted as a response to the threatened internal chaos of users and their attempt to stabilize and maintain their orientation to everyday experience. In so doing, personal stereos become starter motors or fantasy triggers through which users construct forms of experiential certainty in which both space and time becomes predictable. The external world, if reflected on at all, becomes a reflection of the subjective intention of the user. The use of personal stereos demonstrates that embedded in the everyday lifeworld of users is a dialectical tension: the desire to maintain forms of experiential control is expressed precisely through forms of dependency on technologically mediated forms of company. How then should we perceive this mobile technologized site of habitation? It is precisely the constitution of this site that is unreflectively ignored in much literature on the use of communication technologies (Fiske 1989).

Living Inside a Personal Stereo

The ethnographic material presented in the earlier parts of this book demonstrates that personal-stereo users construct conceptual habitats for themselves through which they manage their daily experience. These habitats are mobile and technologically constructed and transforms the user's relationship to representational space. Indeed the two can no longer be easily separated as the site of experience becomes synonymous with representational space through use. I have been arguing throughout this book for the need to evaluate the meanings of those terms that often become mere coat hangers upon which writers drape examples. One such term in need of critical reflection is the 'site' of experience. How then should the site of experience be articulated so as to cast explanatory light upon personal-stereo use?

The present analysis indicates that users display a heightened sensitivity towards being centred and in control of the everyday, both cognitively and spatially. These strategies appear to mask an anxiety concerning the fragility of these states, both in relation to their own cognition and the contingency of the social world through which they move. In the following pages I wish to investigate the meanings attached to notions of 'centredness' in order to fully understand its applicability to the strategies engaged upon by personal-stereo users. I begin with the work of Richard Sennett (1990) who has provided an articulate and historically informed account of strategies of centredness in Western culture. Interestingly he locates 'centredness' as existing in the geography of urban spaces in which sanctuaries were created, initially in the form of churches and later in the bourgeois home itself. These rather material and spatial manifestations of sanctuaries represent a physical zone of 'immunity' between the person either as a member of a congregation or as a member of a family and the world or space beyond. Sennett describes this zone of separation as in a sense being blessed with qualities not attributable to the world beyond. These spaces provide a clarity not available in the world beyond. In inhabiting them urban subjects are perceived of as withdrawing from a world of confusion and instability that lacks adequate definition. Sennett interprets the attempt to create order, stability and control within an 'inner' realm in terms of a progressive 'privatization of experience' embodied in Western culture. By developing this train of thought the use of personal stereos might constitute the last, albeit problematic, refuge of a retreating public subjectivity. Personal-stereo use substitutes or supplements the home, and more recently the car, as a creator of private space, conceptualized phenomenologically, as a 'sanctuary'. Theirs is a technological sanctuary conceptually created or constituted through auditory listening which erects a barrier between the subject and the exterior world.

It is precisely the nature of this technologically constituted site of experience which needs articulation. Sennett leaves the actual 'site' of the 'experiencing subject' as unproblematized and instead concentrates on the interpersonal ramifications of this retreat into inwardness in terms of its consequences on multicultural urban living. He is aware, not so much of technology as constituting the 'quality of touch' (Silverstone) but with attributing the values of individualism to a retreat from the 'touch'. This is because he is primarily concerned with behaviour in 'public' as signifying experientially a cultural set of values encompassed by 'individualism'.

Whilst I am in agreement with Sennett's analysis of a progressive withdrawal from the public, I wish rather to focus precisely upon the nature of a technologized form of the site of experience. The history of technological habitation has hardly been written. Television viewers, for example, have been characterized as increasingly retreating into forms of interior space, yet the constitution of this 'interior space' is invariably left open (Moores 1993). In this context, personal-stereo use might be understood as representing a desire for some kind of 'onto-logical security' (Giddens 1991). However such existentialist notions are often neglectful of the historical contextualization of both the subject and the technological artifact. With this potential criticism in mind I now discuss the work of Gaston Bachelard (1988). He provides an original phenomenological description of the site of experience that can be creatively adapted to shed light on the meanings attached to personal-stereo users' attempts to construct safe urban habitats of experience. Bachelard analyses metaphors of 'enclosure' found in poetry and in doing so points to the phenomenological status and significance of the site of experience intentionally conceived in terms of metaphors of 'home'. His analysis perceptively points to a dialectics of home understood in terms of the polarities of safety and danger. Whilst he fails to provide any historical contextualization of these experiences his analysis can provide a useful contextualization for personal-stereo users' descriptions of the 'site' of experience. His description of 'home' resonates closely with contemporary descriptions of personal stereo experiences as they describe their technologically mediated universe. Personal-stereo users are certainly no poets, but the metaphor of 'home' resonates clearly as a form of phenomenological intentionality in their account of living inside their personal stereos. Bachelard claims that a phenomenology:

> Should therefore have to say how we inhabit our vital space, in accord with all dialectics of life, how we take root, day after day, in a 'corner of the world' . . . All really inhabited space bears the essence of the notion of home. The imagination functions in this direction whenever the human being has found the slightest shelter: we shall see the imagination build 'walls' of impalpable shadows, comfort itself with the illusion of protection . . . A house constitutes a body of images that give mankind proofs or illusions of stability. We are constantly re-imagining its reality . . . A house is imagined as a concentrated being. It appeals to our consciousness of centrality. (Bachelard 1988, p. 4–5)

Bachelard, whilst providing an interesting explanation of the relation-ship of the site (inner experience) to the context of experience (outer experience), tends to create a dichotomy between the two whilst also ignoring the interpersonal nature of habitation so important to the present analysis. Lefebvre is correct in his observation of Bachelard's work when he says that:

> The relationship between Home and Ego, meanwhile borders on identity. The shell, a secret and directly experienced space, for Bachelard epitomises the virtues of human space. (Lefebvre 1991b, p. 121)

However, what I take from Bachelard is his descriptive richness of the phenomenological construction of the site of experience which can be appropriated and used to cast light on the technological constitution of 'home' For Bachelard 'a poem possesses us entirely' and through it we are able to 'experience resonances, sentimental repercussions, reminders of our own past'. The experience of using personal stereos similarly engulfingly absorbs the user directing them into the imaginary reconstruction of their own past. Yet instead of recreating this sense of 'home' in the meditative or imaginary realm constructed out of the 'text', as described by Bachelard, the personal-stereo user does this both in the privacy of listening in the home, a conceptual home within a bricks-and-mortar home, or continually recreates it within the public realm.

Bachelard's construction is a phenomenology of a utopian intentionality, a grand metaphor of escape. In this imaginary escape the subject is free:

> But phenomenology of the imagination . . . demands that images be lived directly, that they be taken as sudden events in life. When the image is new, the world is new. And in reading applied to life, all passivity disappears if we try to become aware of the creative acts of the poet expressing the world, a world that becomes accessible to our daydreaming. (Bachelard 1988, p. 47)

In this act of freedom through the imaginary, space is reconstituted, it 'flees the object nearby and right away it is far off, elsewhere, in the space of elsewhere'(Bachelard 1988, p. 184). Bachelard provides us with a description of the reinscription of space through the imaginary creation of the site of experience as that of a self enclosed 'shell' that freely takes the subject into a freer realm of 'inhabited space'. Bachelard's description of this bears a great resemblance to the dreaming that Rousseau recounts on his solitary walks rather than to today's technologically mediated imaginary space of the personal-stereo user. Bachelard's dreamers dream in silence whereas it is precisely this silence that personal-stereo users fear. They tend to feel isolated with no sound. Their home has to have sound, not the sound of the street, the chaos of urban sounds but their own controlled, predicable technological sounds. Their own technologically mediated sound constitutes their 'inhabited space' which correspondingly transcends the sounds of 'geographical space'. Ernst Bloch's early description of the intimate and utopian space of 'habitation' is in tune with Bachelard's:

Here too the fun of being invisible ourselves. We seek a corner, it protects and conceals. It feels good in a narrow space, but we know we can do what we want there. A woman relates, 'I wish I could be under the cupboard, I want to live there' . . . The hidden boy is also breaking out. He is searching for what is far away, even though he shuts himself in, it is just that in breaking free he has girded himself round and round with walls. All the better if the hiding place is mobile. (Bloch 1986, p. 22–3)

The place where one can be oneself is articulated here in terms of physical separation. Of escaping to be oneself. Adorno, in contrast to this, whilst agreeing with the subjective sentiment concentrates on the historical process of the 'colonization' of the 'site' of experience by the social network in which:

We might conceive a series leading from the man who cannot work without the blare of the radio to the one that kills time and paralyses loneliness by filling his ears with the illusion of 'being with' no matter what. (Adorno 1991, p. 16)

Adorno points to the problematic nature of constructing a 'site' of experience within representational space together with the problematic nature of the phenomenological construction of subjective intentionality. In Adorno's analysis the subject dresses up his site which is actually an 'illusory realm' filled out by society. The impulse to create this 'illusory realm', however, is where I interpret Adorno's analysis as being in agreement with both Bloch's and Bachelard's. It is precisely the status of this utopian 'imaginary' realm that needs articulating.

Adorno points to the very specific spatial redistribution of experience through technology which manufactures states of 'we-ness' in contemporary culture. In analysing personal-stereo users' habitation of space and place I have thrown light upon the dialectical nature of this process. Personal-stereo users construct their urban experience through a privately experienced auditized soundworld. Through the construction of auratic states of 'we-ness' which signifies an intimate and consuming form of mediated 'company', personal-stereo use is understood through a negative dialectic whereby users withdraw into public forms of solitude. As such, users are both isolated and accompanied. Their accompaniment is constituted by the mediated messages of the products of the 'culture industry'. The above analysis points to these states of 'being with' as being appropriately understood as part of an historical and cultural trajectory highlighted in the early work of Critical Theorists. Intrinsic to users' management of the spaces of habitation is their management of time, the precondition for all experience.

Managing Time

In Chapter Five I demonstrated how personal-stereo users managed their day with great precision, and in doing so the present analysis casts doubt on the usefulness of discretely partitioning everyday life into the categories of free and unfree, leisure or work. Rather, personal-stereo use indicates that these categories themselves need to understood both dialectically and historically. However, in much sociological literature time is regularly represented dichotomously as either 'leisure' or 'free' time and then contrasted and compared to 'work' time. Equally, as noted previously in this chapter, it is common to decontextualize everyday behaviour from the wider structural constraints within which it is placed, which results in an unreflective engagement with those categories.[3] The analysis of personal-stereo use indicated that it is more accurate to understand use as an attempt to create 'free time' together with 'free areas' of experience. However, historically notions of 'free time, have invariably meant time away from work, with 'identity' work being situated within the realm of the 'unfree', in the realm of productive activity (Marx 1964). More recently the significance of the role of work has become progressively displaced with identity work becoming located in the private realms of consumption and leisure.[4] In contrast to both of the above positions personal-stereo use appears to blur any reified distinction that might be made concerning the division of people's 'lifeworld' into dichotomous realms of 'work' and 'leisure'. Personal-stereo users rather attempt to reclaim the significance of their experience of time precisely in those lifeworld areas that have previously been perceived to be of little significance in the literature on time, identity and experience.

Personal-stereo use demonstrates the extension of scriptwriting into areas of everyday life previously considered to be insignificant. The ritualized journey and the pressing demands of the everyday come with a recognition that the cyclical and linear components of the day constitute either a threat or an unacceptable incursion to their everyday life. Users' experiences are rather understood in terms of their desire to operationalize a 'compensatory metaphysics' in which time is transformed and experience heightened through its technologically mediated management.

Both reproduced sound and the artifact itself are themselves products of the culture industry and this makes the relationship between technology and the construction and role of 'free areas' of personal stereo experience problematic. Whilst Cohen and Taylor point to the dialectic construction of everyday experience they nevertheless fall back on dichotomous distinctions of daily experience:

> Now for many parts of our daily life, the situation may appear unscripted. Our journey to work, for example, does not involve any necessity to name actors or plot behaviour. However, as soon as we come into contact with others in those spheres of life which we consider as 'projects', 'key areas', 'life plans' – areas of home, work, leisure, politics – then we are more likely to enter into miniature dramas where defining, naming, plotting, are at a premium. (Cohen and Taylor 1976, p. 71)

In contrast to this, personal-stereo users rewrite scripts continually within areas of the everyday that were previously assumed to be 'unscripted'. Scripts become imposed upon those mundane and routine periods of empty time. Alternatively, scripts are extended into linear time in order to delay involvement in the 'bad' script of unpleasurable but inevitable reality. Users need to re-appropriate time and script in as many activities as possible. Yet an analysis of the everyday constructed around the reification of private (meaningful) and public (meaningless, unscripted) misunderstands significant features of the constitution of those very practices. For example Cohen and Taylor argue that:

> We can happily become lost in the anonymous ritualised journeys to and from work, for we know that this surrenders nothing that is important to ourselves. We do not live or do identity work in these places. Real life is elsewhere. (Cohen and Taylor 1976, p. 50)

Personal stereo use implies a rather different story. The ritualized journey and the pressing demands of the everyday come with the recognition that both the cyclical and linear constitute a threat. Identity work is thus continually enacted by users. Alternatively some users reinscribe the ritual of everyday practices with their own chosen, more meaningful set of 'rituals'. What becomes clear is that users often believe that 'real life is elsewhere' and use personal stereos to reclaim the significance of the present. The feeling that 'something' should be happening, that the user's life is significant in the here and now, is part and parcel of the incursion and constitution of time through the consumption of culture-industry products within the everyday.

Within this context personal-stereo use might be seen as an everyday 'strategy of dissociation' (Cohen and Taylor 1976) whereby users operationalize role-distancing strategies in imaginative forms of consumption that they perceive to be both 'personalizing' and liberating. Cohen and Taylor, like Lefebvre and Adorno, view these strategies as products of the very system to be escaped from:

> By our diligent use of escape routes we seek to construct in our minds that which does not appear to us in the world. We attempt to create free areas in which our individuality having been rested from society, may now enjoy a certain immunity. The ability of society to co-opt, infiltrate and subvert those very areas which we had hoped to hold sacred for the attainment of meaning, progress and self has been increased through this century. (Cohen and Taylor 1976, p. 225)

This dialectic of control and resistance articulated in everyday life is in need of theoretical articulation. The structure of everyday life is constituted by rhythms imposed upon subjects by system world formations in the everyday lifeworld of subjects. Personal-stereo users' lifeworlds are thus built upon routines and repetition which are both historically and culturally conditioned as are the structurally conditioned nature of 'escape' routines found within culture. From this point of view users operationalize prescribed forms of individualism which condition subjective forms of escape from routines deemed threatening to their status as an individual user. Critical Theorists were amongst the first to analyse and articulate the formation of structurally determined forms of escape through the constitution of the the 'culture industry' (Horkheimer and Adorno 1973).

> The escape from everyday drudgery which the whole culture industry promises may be compared to the daughter's abduction in the cartoon: the father is holding the ladder in the dark. The paradise offered by the culture industry is the same old drudgery. Both escape and elopement lead back to the starting point. (Horkheimer and Adorno 1973, p. 142)

However, the above represents a premature foreclosure of meaning. Adorno's pessimism should not be taken literally but rather as a dialectical moment in the analysis of everyday life. Throughout my analysis of personal-stereo use notions of experiential saturation and colonization have vied with those concerned with mediation and the expression of utopian aspirations. The use of personal stereos appears both to saturate the experience of the everyday and to mediate it. To saturate implies a filling up, a taking in, an all-engulfing process or alternatively a taking over whereby mediation implies a more active process of filtering and adjustment. I take the position that the relationship between technology and experience in the 'lifeworld' can be construed as two moments in the dialectic of experience, that these 'are the torn halves of an integral freedom, to which however they do not add up' (Wolin 1994).

By developing the often fragmentary concepts introduced by early Critical Theorists I am able to articulate the ways in which users' resistance to colonization within their lifeworld might be understood. Through the operationalizing of notions of 'compensatory metaphysics' and 'exact fantasy' together with Lefebvre's understanding of the phenomenology of experiential time a set of useful tools are created in articulating a dialectic of colonization and mediation. Throughout the analysis the imaginative strategies of resistance have been understood as being grounded in the commonplace activities of the everyday. Whilst users might be said to experience the social totality as being increasingly deterritoralized and transacted in their private networks of individualized consumption this does not merely imply that 'commodities and industries now realise themselves in human beings'. Experience is rather usefully perceived of as being 'at once pre-organized and unorganised'. (Negt and Kluge 1993, p. 6)

The construction of experience through personal-stereo use can be understood dialectically whereby the products of culture, in the form of music listened to and the artifact of the personal stereo, are inscribed into any public or private environment and increasingly incorporate both the private realms of users' experiences and the context of their everyday life. Whilst these products increasingly constitute the lifeworld of the subject population there remains a disjunction between the subject and the object of the culture industry that produces a necessary failure of total subsumption or incorporation of all elements of the everyday into that system world. This point is highlighted in the dialectical relation of forms of 'compensatory metaphysics' incorporated through forms of aestheticized experience that take their form in notions of narrativized experience within personal-stereo use. However, this experience is also problematic in the sense that the imaginary lies within the remit of the consciousness industry. In this sense, are the imaginative strategies used by users merely culturally prescribed? I argue that the creativity often displayed in personal-stereo use often arises precisely through those formulaic modes of experience in which users make their daily life habitable. Negt and Kluge, whilst recognizing the ambivalent nature and role of the imaginary, argue that:

> experience and fantasy production are far richer than the consciousness industry can represent, the possibility for organising this experience of fantasy is limited structurally. (Negt and Kluge 1993, p. 170)

The role of fantasy embodied in personal-stereo use demonstrates the success of a range of strategies; habitable space does indeed become more manageable for users. Personal stereos function within this scenario as a form of 'unburdening', freeing up time to be filled by alternative communication technologies. Free time becomes time to be consumed through the management of ever broadening areas of daily life in which users can 'be themselves'. Personal-stereo users can be understood as pitting themselves against the 'realm of the eversame' (Adorno) or the 'ever-always-the-same' (Benjamin). In doing so personal stereos dress up their experience as a form of intimate communion with the world. The narrative, mood or thought processes of the user mediated through their personal stereo changes the significance of experienced time. Underlying this process is the desire to manage time in a manner that either solves the problematic nature of mundane experience through a process of 'reclaiming' time or through an imaginary form of control by which the contingency of experience in public can be managed. Personal-stereo users invariably describe 'needing' their machine to cope with time experienced on their own. The desire to fill up time in this way appears to be historically embedded and situated within a technological milieu that enables not only the solving, but also the creation of this situation. In doing so personal-stereo users redraw the dichotomous categories of public and private; leisure and work in their everyday world. The everyday is defined critically as being unable to provide the significance or meaning desired by users. Personal-stereo use become a temporary, yet everyday, method of dealing with this disjunction.

> The everyday is situated at the intersection of two modes of repetition: the cyclical, which dominates nature, and the linear which dominates the processes known as 'rational' . . . In modern life the repetitive gestures tends to mask and to crush the cycles. The everyday imposes its own monotony. It is the invariable constant of the variation it envelops. The

days follow one another and resemble one another, and yet – and here lies the contradiction at the heart of everydayness – everything changes. But the change is programmed: obsolescence is planned. Production anticipates reproduction; production produces change in such a way as to superimpose the impression of speed on that of monotony. (Osborne 1995, p. 196)

This emancipatory moment in the flux of the everyday is highlighted in Lefebvre's phenomenologically informed analysis of time and experience in which the structure of the everyday is left open, forever unfinished. Lefebvre articulates this in his late work under the notion of 'rhythm analysis' where notions of 'cyclical' and 'linear' time are interwoven:

Time is projected onto space through measures, uniformizing it and emerging in things and products. The apparent reversibility of time through the products of the everyday gives us a feeling of contentedness, constructing a rampart against the tragic and death. The tragic exists outside dailiness but it irrupts within it . . . Rhythm analysis is the means by which we understand the struggle against time within time itself. (Lefebvre 1996, p. 31)

Personal stereo use, in this context, is understood as projecting time, the time of music reception, onto the space of the journey thus enabling the user to create forms of 'habitable experience'. In doing so users gain a sense of personal control over time and space and are able to sustain their mood precisely by keeping it 'suspended' in time. Personal-stereo use can be accurately perceived as a temporary wager against the experience of cyclical time. However, in considering the status of this wager an open-ended phenomenology of time would indicate that user's lifeworld experiences cannot coincide completely with the systems world. Yet this is coupled with the recognition that utopian moments of opposition are framed within the consumption of culture that is itself being rebelled against.

Notes

1. It is important to recognise that the role of the personal stereo is not neutral in relation to its everyday use. Due weight should be given to the constitution of ideological dispositions embodied in forms of usage which

appear to be intimately tied to those Western values of individualism, utilitarianism and instrumentalism which are manifested in both the design and uses of the personal stereo in the realm of the everyday. Akio Morita, the then chairman of the Sony Corporation, demonstrates this point with the following remark:

> At my home, my children were always playing their stereos in their rooms, making my happy home a noisy one. In the car as well, they played their stereo loudly. But once they went outdoors, there were no machines to play their music. Of course I did see on the street some youngsters carrying big cassette systems on their shoulders, but these were too loud and heavy. So with these ideas in our heads, we thought that the creation of a small stereo cassette player with lightweight headphones had the potential to fill a yet unrecognised market need. (Ohsone 1988, p. 5)

Morita's observation concerning the integral role of music in youth culture is tied to notions of the creation of 'new lifestyles' embedded in the products of the culture industry. Within this scenario the personal stereo answers a latent desire, already firmly established in patterns of consumption; to listen to music wherever and whenever the consumer desires. This observation unreflectively incorporates an orientation to experience that is both instrumentalist and privatized. Morita's remark is also, implicitly, a negative judgment on the role and significance of the urban in the constitution of everyday experience.

These values become operative in the very design of personal stereos. For example, designers created personal stereo headphones that wrapped around the head to be used for solitary use. Later, discrete and more aesthetically pleasing headpieces that fitted directly into the ears were designed only to be replaced by large, very visible, headphones that wrap around the head. If the public realm is increasingly negated then the need for discretion evaporates.

2. Silverstone describes television as having an ontological and phenomenological reality related to 'television's veritable dailyness'. The everyday presence of television becomes, he argues, either a part of, or a substitution for, the securities offered in the past by institutions such as the family, neighbourhood, community or nation which have:

> historically been the containers of, and provided the resources for, our ability to sustain that defence (against anxiety). That ability itself is grounded in turn on our ability, within the activities of our daily lives, to preserve a sense of continuity and reliability of things, to provide, as best we can, the necessary distance between us and the various threats to that continuity, either by denying them completely or by absorbing them, in one way or another, into the fabric of our life. (Silverstone 1994, p. 1)

Television use, in its habitualness, fulfils this function precisely at a time when these traditional forms of association are decreasingly present in everyday urban experience. Silverstone argues that television viewing replaces locality to some extent with the medium being invested with trust in the sense that it becomes a focal point for feelings of security:

> Television accompanies us as we wake up, as we breakfast, as we have our tea and as we drink in bars. It comforts us when we are alone. It helps us sleep. It gives us pleasure, it bores us and sometimes challenges us. It provides us with opportunities to be both sociable and solitary. (Silverstone 1994, p. 3)

The above description appears to mirror personal stereo use in its habitualness. The role of the auditory appears to be of greater significance to many personal-stereo users than television viewing although it might well be seen to perform a similar purpose. That users take their personal stereos 'out' with them might merely be seen to be an extension of television use within the experiential objectives described above by Silverstone. Indeed mobile televisions are increasingly used on transatlantic aircraft, in American airports and Greyhound coach stations. The world experienced through technology is a world 'colonized' in Silverstone's analysis:

> My argument, in relation to television, is that precisely because television has colonised these basic levels of social reality (the relation between consciousness, self and social encounters) that we need to understand it better . . . But this capacity to provide a permanent presence and, in doing so, a colonisation of potential space is not simply a function of the quality of the technology [television]. Many technologies, particularly communicating or informing technologies do indeed have the capacity to generate a degree of dependence, security and attachment in a similar way to television; each case is potentially both creative and addictive.(Silverstone 1994, p. 4–15)

Silverstone frames the question in terms of a dialectical tension between the colonized lifeworld as being both potentially addictive and creative.

3. This is demonstrated in the work of Cohen and Taylor (1976) but is also apparent in the work of Ang (1985), Fiske (1989) and Hebdige (1988).

4. These social processes were mirrored, albeit descriptively, in much postwar British empirical sociology that proclaimed the virtues of instrumentalist approaches to work in which work and leisure became polar opposites. By the 1960s significant time, time to be 'oneself' was increasingly located in activities in the home or perhaps leisure pursuits (Goldthorpe and Lockwood 1968/9). Thus the parcelling up of time was accepted as given, with work being portrayed as having no meaning in contrast to home life which was saturated with it.

This dichotomous model of lifeworld activities became the norm in sociological accounts of experience. As such public areas of life were already becoming subordinate to accounts which celebrated the privatized nature of the home as a source of all value. When behaviour in public was discussed it increasingly took the form of an analysis of consumer pursuits such as 'shopping in the mall' which often represented an unreflective description of the furtherance of the aestheticization of mundane everyday life attuned to the 'empowerment' of consumers.

Aestheticizing Everyday Life:
A Critique

The empirical phenomena, which are understood by proponents of postmodernism as the expression of an increase in aesthetic freedom, must be interpreted largely as the negative consequence of a breakdown in traditional relations of recognition, in particular those established in industrial societies. In this respect, many of the works which today are undertaken in the interest of a diagnosis of the present era point indirectly to a condition in our society which I would describe as a crisis in the structure of the social relations of recognition.

A. Honneth, *The Fragmentary World of the Social*

In this final chapter I address the use of personal stereos in relation to the aestheticization of everyday life. Aestheticization is a strategy embedded in the use of a range of communication technologies. The status of this experience has, however, been too frequently discussed in non-relational or falsely neutral terms in urban and cultural literature whereas I have been arguing that to aestheticize everyday life is to engage in forms of social asymmetry that are not at all 'neutral'. There has, I feel, been a conceptual slippage in many discussions of the aestheticization of everyday life. Simply put, modes of aesthetic appreciation concerning looking at a painting or in listening to a piece of music need to be distinguished from aestheticizing the practices of everyday life. Bauman, despite his interest in the nature of 'moral' spaces in the city nonetheless describes aesthetic modes of urban experience as being harmless and pleasurable due to their 'inconsequentiality':

> Aesthetically, the city space is a spectacle in which the amusement value overrides all other considerations. (Bauman, 1993 p. 168)

It is, however, by no means apparent that this activity is so inconsequential. For example, the strategies undertaken by personal-stereo users suggest that the motivations involved in the aestheticization process are rather more complex than Bauman suggests. The following personal-stereo user's account demonstrates the problematic and ambiguous nature of aestheticizing everyday life:

> But when I'm out I'm looking for things that I see – in the world, human interaction – beautiful things that I think can touch my soul – you know, that certain sound at a certain time and it will just move me to tears – and it is filmic. But it's very real. I'm not seeing something that isn't there. That woman in the street. She's really there. She doesn't have anywhere to sleep. but it's because I'm listening to music that's really tender it moves me even more. (Jay: interview number 33)

Jay aestheticizes her experience through musical accompaniment. The experience is described as having pathos in the same way as if she were watching a film or a television programme on poverty from the comfort of her home. Implied in the above description is that if the music is not right, then somehow the woman in the street, who is really there, will not have the same presence. The situation becomes 'real' if it is filmic. The 'subject' of this aesthetic appropriation, however, remains untouched, as she merely constitutes an aestheticized fragment contributing to the user's sense of urban narrative. The narcissistic recreation of meaning in terms of a heightening of the individual's sense of meaning through music is a significant aspect of personal stereo experience. This example is a good place to begin the evaluation of the meanings attached to technologically mediated forms of social aestheticization. Important to the following analysis is the contextualizing of this activity. Personal-stereo users engage in activities 'taken out' of the living room and placed within the street. This type of personal-stereo use becomes an exemplar for my critique of forms of 'mobile privatization' undertaken later in this chapter.

In the present analysis of personal-stereo use I understand strategies of aestheticization to be dialectical inasmuch as they are both utopian, and hence transcendent in character, as well as being located firmly in alienating and objectifying cultural predispositions that deny difference within culture (Sennett 1990). The dialectical and ambiguous role of technology in the aestheticization process is highlighted in the work of Adorno in which he discusses the utopian function of new technologies in everyday life. In the following quote Adorno is in discussion with Ernst Bloch concerning the status and meaning of the term 'utopian' with regard to contemporary experience. He refers to a poem by Wilhelm Busch (quoted in Bloch 1988, p. 2) which I reproduce in full:

> Just arrived in this region.
> Much more than very rich
> In his hand a telescope
> Came a mister by the name of Pief
> 'Why shouldn't I look.'
> Said he, 'onto the distance as I walk?
> It's also beautiful somewhere else
> And here I am at any rate.'

In this example the experience of distance is transformed by the technological artifact: the telescope. Adorno appropriates and transforms the original impulse of the poem in order to articulate the role of technology in delivering the magical or utopian aspirations of people. Importantly, utopian elements are perceived to be cast into the formation and design of the technology which is tied to a set of cultural imperatives at the outset. In this instance the technology of the telescope transforms the ability to traverse distance just as television, the internet or the mobile phone do in their own individual ways. The previous inability of subjects to accomplish these feats coupled with the aspiration to negate distance constitutes the utopian element or moment in the use of the technology. However Adorno perceives this utopian impulse as being thrown back upon itself due to its failure to realize itself in the realm of the totality of social relations. Aestheticization thus comes about due to the failure of utopian aspirations to realize themselves in any other way. Marxism and Aristotelianism are thus coupled in Adorno's refusal to abstract particulars from the generality. Adorno points to the paradoxical nature of aesthetic experience which cannot be realized in any other way:

> Numerous so-called utopian dreams – for example, television, the possibility of travelling to other planets, moving faster than sound – have been fulfilled. However, insofar as these dreams have been realised, they operate as though the best thing about them has been forgotten – one is not happy about them. As they have been realised, the dreams themselves have assumed a peculiar character of sobriety, of boredom. (Adorno in Bloch 1988, p. 2)

Adorno describes experience as both appropriating and reified whilst the utopian moment atrophies into boredom. It is this turning back in on itself rather than the 'instrumentality' of the technology which is significant in Adorno's analysis:

> This word begins to assume a horrifying meaning today in the realisation of technological utopias, that 'here I am at any rate' also takes possession of the 'somewhere else.' (Adorno in Bloch, 1988, p. 3)

The meaning of this colonisation of the 'somewhere else' by the user through the mediating influence of technology is centrally important to my analysis of personal-stereo use. In Adorno's analysis a dialectic is formed between the power-infused technological experience of users and a resulting social impotence which is transmuted into a process of subjective aestheticization. This process need not necessarily be contradictory. The disjunction between the will to power and its social frustration produce a range of managing procedures whereby the 'somewhere else' is consumed or appropriated by the 'here and now'. For Adorno, space becomes subjectivized in the act of consumption, thus acting to fetishize immediate experience. The instrumentality of the technological reformulation of the lifeworld becomes reified in its inability to realize its utopian impulse. This results in a privatization of the impulse to the exclusion of any contradiction. As Adorno states:

> They need and demand what has been palmed off on them. They overcome the feeling of impotence that creeps over them in the face of monopolistic production by identifying themselves with the inescapable product. (Adorno 1992, p. 288)

Listening to music thus becomes integrative. Paradoxically the desire and experience of control becomes local and inner directed. The consumer:

> can stabilise its identity only through continual exclusion of all sense experience that threatens to impair the direct pursuit of the principle of control. (Honneth 1993, p. 45)

Yet there remains a residue of dissatisfaction in Adorno's account. One 'is not happy with' the unfulfilled expectation, and powerlessness is experienced as ever possible. There is thus a dichotomy between the colonization of the lifeworld and the experiencing subject that doesn't merely add up to a mimetic relationship but rather points to a remainder:

What the culture industry presents people with in their free time, if my conclusions are not too hasty, is indeed consumed and accepted, but with a kind of reservation, in the same way that even the most naive theatre or film goers do not simply take what they behold there for real. Perhaps one can go further and say it is not quite believed in. It is obvious that the integration of consciousness and free time has not completely succeeded. The real interests of individuals are still strong enough to resist, within certain limits, total inclusion. This would concur with the social prediction that a society, whose inherent contradictions persist undiminished, cannot integrate even in consciousness. (Adorno 1991, p. 170)

Adorno implies that there is a disjunction between the socially constructed lifeworld and the experiencing subject, yet his allusion to modes of contestation seem to rest unhappily with his more systematic statements on the power of modern communication technology to preform and constitute desire. The historical case for the fetishization of subjective experience and the negation or dismissal of the public sphere together with the flattening out of experience, the experience of difference, prefigures Marcuse's notion of 'one dimensional experience' (Marcuse 1972b). The historical distance between the telescope user, the television watcher and the personal-stereo user appears, more often than not, to be described in terms of the colonization of lifeworlds. In this scenario the world and experience are perceived as becoming directly mediated by the manufactured content of 'media messages' which transform the 'site' of experience. Should personal-stereo use be understood merely as one advanced example of this tendency? In previous chapters I discussed the manner in which users lived with and through communication technologies and how our sensory expectations developed in conjunction with the use of artifacts like television, radio, the computer and so on. The habitual desire to aestheticize experience is both learnt through the use of these technologies and made achievable through their use. Personal-stereo use has both extended the facility and empowered it through the specifically auditory nature of the medium.

Technology and the Power of the 'Look'

Personal stereos transform the power of the user over the social just as other forms of communication technology empower users in a host of other social situations from the home to the office. Personal-stereo users feel empowered in much the same way as film spectators might. If film spectators are in a position of 'imaginary omnipotence' then personal-stereo use might be interpreted as generalizing this impulse into the street through the technology of the artifact. This indeed connects personal-stereo use to the camera. The subject, as the omnipotent centre of vision, transforms the world at will through the camera:

> I am the camera's eye. I am the machine which shows you the world as I alone see it. starting from today, I am free of human immobility. I am perpetual movement. I approach and draw away from things – I climb on them – I am on the head of galloping horses – I burst at full speed into a crowd – I run before running soldiers – I throw myself down on my back – I rise up with aeroplanes – I fall and I fly at one with bodies falling and rising through the air. (quoted in Virilio 1989, p. 11)

This description is not very far removed from the descriptions of empowerment provided by personal-stereo users. Just as the camera is described as an omnipotent extension of consciousness and intensionality, so mirrored in this, albeit with less flamboyant language, are personal-stereo users who use music as an extension of their senses and intentionality in public. Within this form of technologically mediated control the status and constitution of this experience becomes paramount. The urban was described by users as not being experienced 'filmicly' without the use of a personal stereo. To experience something 'filmicly' means necessarily therefore to experience it technologically. Benjamin in discussing the camera and the 'look', develops an analysis that focuses upon forms of asymmetry that are built into new forms of technology:

> In daguerreotypy was the prolonged look of the camera, since it records our likeness without returning our gaze. But looking at someone carries the implicit expectation that our look will be returned by the object of our gaze. Where this expectation is met (which in the case of thought processes, can apply equally to the look of the eye of the mind and to a glance pure and simple), there is an experience of aura to the fullest extent. 'Perceptibility,' as Novalis puts it, 'is a kind of attentiveness.' Experience of the aura thus rests on the transposition of a response common in human relationships to the relationship between the inanimate or natural object and man. The person we look at, or who feels he is being looked at, looks at us in return. (Benjamin 1973a, p. 184)

The hard glare of the camera lens does not return the gaze, rather it defines. Its power is essentially asymmetrical. It forbids aura as aura resides in the construction of the returned gaze (intentionally). For example one might say the painting speaks to me, but one cannot say that about the camera lens. Thus begins for Benjamin the experiential training in reconstituting looking and being looked at, both empirically and intentionally. Susan Buck-Morss comments:

> Finally the cinema epitomises, in the very structure of the apparatus, a decline of the human capability to return the gaze, a historical experience to have lost the ability to look. (Buck-Morss 1991, p. 204)

The power basis of the experiencing subject is thus changed in relation to social space and its inhabitants, as Hansen notes:

> What I wish to suggest is that the emergence of cinema spectatorship is profoundly intertwined with the transformation of the public sphere in particular the gendered itineraries of everyday life and leisure. (Hansen 1991, p. 2)

Thus the cinema continues the process begun by the camera in the construction of the isolated voyeur and by implication creates the precondition for non-reciprocal gazing. The asymmetrical nature of the cinematic gaze is brought out in Benjamin's discussion of the relationship of the film actor and the camera:

> The film actor lacks the opportunity of the stage actor to adjust to the audience during his performance, since he does not present his perform-ance to the audience in person. This permits the audience to take the position of the critic, without experiencing any personal contact with the actor. The audience's identification with the actor is really an identification with the camera. Consequently the audience take the position of the camera. (Benjamin 1973a, p. 222)

Thus the preconditions for the aestheticization of experience is put at the disposal of the subject. But this aestheticization is implicitly power laden and opens the door to an analysis of contemporary forms of asymmetry and control by which to understand the nature of personal-stereo use. What do these observations permit us to say about the aestheticization of experience articulated through both personal-stereo use and other forms of communication technology? It is here that I take issue with the consensual framework within which aestheticization is understood both within the urban everyday (*flânerie*) and within the use of communication technologies of which personal-stereo use is merely one example. In order to do so I focus critically upon Williams's understanding of 'mobile privatization' which I take to be the theoretical paradigm underlying most work in the field of communication technology and everyday life.

Mobile Privatization and the Colonization of Urban Space

New mediums of communication technology have reconstituted the relationship of domestic or private life to the world beyond it and in so doing have reconstituted or transformed both human sensibilities and social structures (Silverstone 1994, p. 92). In this scenario the media may well function as a form of mediation between anxiety and reassurance:

> Real dependence and illusory control that I have already begun to identify as lying at the heart of an understanding of contemporary life. (Silverstone 1994, p. 54)

It is precisely Silverstone's understanding of 'illusory control' that is important in the present discussion of aestheticization. Silverstone introduces the notion of 'home and reach' to signify the relationship of experiencing the 'public' within the 'private'. He points to the 'quality' of the relation between the subject and the 'other' as being significant. In his work the technological extension of experience does not necessarily signify 'control' but is understood as being merely 'aesthetic'. This locates Silverstone's work within a theoretical framework similar to that provided by Critical Theorists in their discussion of technology and experience. I in turn wish to situate notions of aesthetic 'control' in an understanding of the relational nature of urban experience understood as a 'moral' space. In doing so I draw upon Honneth's understanding of the social dynamics involved in recognition, Adorno's work on states of 'we-ness', and upon Silverstone's articulation of 'home and reach' which I contrast to the role of technology in the spacing and placing of experience found in the work of Williams and others where the qualitative and relational character of experience tends to be discounted. In the work of Williams technology is perceived of as assisting both in a mobile existence and a

home-centred one defined by Williams in terms of 'mobile privatization':

> I can't find an ordinary term for it, which is why I have to call it one of
> the ugliest phrases I know: 'mobile privatisation'. It is private. It involves
> a good deal of evident consumption. Much of it centred on the home
> itself. The dwelling place. At the same time it is not a retreating
> privatisation, of a deprived kind, because what it especially confers is an
> unexampled mobility . . . It is not living in a cut off way, not in a shell
> that is just stuck. It is a shell you can take with you, which you can fly
> with to places that previous generations could never imagine visiting.
> (Williams 1977, p. 171)

In Williams's description television becomes a window on the world
whilst mobile privatization refers to the subject's experience of 'travelling' into the public whilst still remaining in their own private realm.
Williams's observation is usefully contrasted with Adorno's discussion
of the telescope user. Whilst Adorno teases out the dialectical nature
of this experience, Williams's description is merely literal and romantic.
He describes users as travelling and learning about the world through
acts of private consumption. The dwelling place as such is filled with a
mediated public world which is increasingly colonized, to use Silverstone's phrase. Inherent in Williams's account is a progressiveness
embodying a 'freedom' to travel through users' habitation of 'mobile
shells' whilst they in fact remain geographically immobile. Williams
describes this unambiguously as being both useful and virtuous. The
qualitative nature of 'home and reach' in these mediated forms of
experience is seen as unproblematic. It is, however, precisely at this
point that Williams's use of the terms 'mobile privatization' and
'unexampled mobility' becomes problematic as tools describing or
enabling an adequate understanding of the relationship between
technology, aesthetic experience and place. This inadequacy is highlighted in Moores's accommodation and use of William's terminology
to understand the significance of media technologies in people's
everyday lives:

> It is necessary for us to ask about the ways in which technology serves
> to 'mediate' between private and public worlds – connecting domestic
> spaces with spheres of information and entertainment that stretch well
> beyond the confines of family and locality. Communication technologies
> have, I will argue, played an important part in the symbolic construction

of 'home' – whilst simultaneously providing household members with an opportunity to 'travel' elsewhere, and to imagine themselves as members of wider cultural communities at a national and transnational level... The multiple ownership of television sets allows household members to make independent journeys to distant destinations and locate themselves within different collectivities. (Moores 1993, p. 22–3)

The relationship between technology, space and experience becomes flattened out into a functionalist account of appropriation based upon the imaginary journeys of the consuming subject. The language of 'community', 'distant destination', 'independent journey', 'different collectivities' is hauled out in a manner that fails to address adequately the constitution of these terms as 'interactional' forms. It rather couches these terms and the experience underlying them within an unreflective discourse of individualism and freedom in which the 'site' of experience is used phenomenologically with no attention given to the constitution of this site. The ambiguous nature of experiencing in a largely aesthetic manner through the mediated messages of the culture industry remain uninvestigated. Williams's television viewers might equally be seen as flattening out experience through its very aestheticization. The experience of the 'other' becoming a function of the desire of the viewer, absorbed in their mimetic desire to both manage and negate difference. These strategies have been demonstrated quite clearly in those personal stereo accounts that stress the aestheticization of experience. I am not claiming that all use fits into this category, merely that the aestheticization of experience is one important strategy embodied in the use of communication technologies and that these strategies are not neutral in their regard to the moral spacings of urban culture. What is required, I am suggesting, is the recognition of a negative dialectic at the heart of Western aestheticizing strategies through which experience is both managed and contingency denied. The present analysis of personal-stereo use demonstrates just what such an analysis might look like.

Personal-Stereo Use: The Dialectic of Aestheticization

The aestheticization practices of personal-stereo users are best understood dialectically as strategies of retreating into pleasurable and managed modes of habitation. Personal-stereo use gives insight into the nature of the subjective organization of experience through the use of forms of technology together with an understanding of the nature of the social embodied in strategies of recognition. Embedded

in these strategies are the ambiguous cultural imperatives of constructed
and mediated forms of 'individualism' which can be partially understood through the work of Sennett and applied culturally in terms of
the appropriation and colonization of space and time via the work of
Adorno, Benjamin, Lefebvre and Honneth.

Embedded in the everyday lifeworld of users is a dialectical tension:
the desire to maintain forms of experiential control is expressed
precisely through forms of dependency on technologically mediated
forms of company. User strategies exist within a range of prefabricated
and technologically reproduced meanings. Whilst these meanings,
which are individualized, are not necessarily prescriptive, they form a
constituent part of the site of experience within which the subject
challenges the ever-present linear commodified time through subjective, privatized and individualized appropriations of these self same
commodifications.[1] The findings of the present study pose the dialectical result of such strategies arguing that technologized experience in
the form of personal-stereo use embodies a fetishization of experience
in a double sense: on the one hand in the technologization of
experience and on the other hand in the colonizing properties of the
aesthetic embodied in much use. Experience is made 'real' or is
heightened only through technologized appropriation. Users construct
or live within auratic space embodying feelings of 'monumentalization'
in which experience is cognitively brought under control. As such,
personal- stereo use signifies the minimalization of the social through
a reconstituted 'imaginary' social inhabited within personal stereo
space.[2] If indeed 'morality is embedded in everyday social practice'
(Honneth 1995b, p. xiv) as Honneth claims, then personal-stereo use
demonstrates the dialectical nature of urban desires for forms of
connectedness or 'community'. Urban space is saturated with an
aestheticized communion of an imaginary, transcendent and non
problematic 'we-ness' conforming to the desires of users whose 'reality'
is experienced through the exclusion of contradiction – the denial of
the 'other' or its aestheticization.

The social construction of the aesthetic is directly related to forms
of social recognition. Personal-stereo users mediate the 'other' in terms
of their own narcissistically orientated intention. The description of
this experience might be more accurately described as 'culturally
solipsistic travelling' . At one extreme, use might be described as a state
of cultural autism defined as 'absorption in imaginative activity directed
by the thinker's wishes, with loss of contact with reality'(Silverstone
1994, p. 54). Honneth argues that the 'struggle for the establishment

of relations of mutual recognition' is a precondition for self-realization itself. He situated the postmodern move to aestheticization as reflecting this trend, arguing that:

> The empirical phenomena, which are understood by proponents of postmodernism as the expression of an increase in aesthetic freedom, must be interpreted largely as the breakdown in traditional relations of recognition. (Honneth 1995b p. xxiii)

Rather than seeing personal-stereo use as reflecting some kind of crisis in everyday relations of recognition, I am more concerned with the qualitative nature of forms of relational experience. Personal-stereo use appears to demonstrate the redundancy of the urban and difference in the everyday life of users and its replacement by the mediated sounds of the culture industry as a site of identity maintenance. Its attractiveness to the user is that it poses no opposition to the assimilatory desire of the subject who is placed comfortably within in the auditory sounds of the personal stereo. Any dialectical account of the role of technology in the experiential appropriation of space and place should imply not merely a cognitive approach to experience but also one which joins an understanding of the aesthetic nature of experience to one concerning the nature of moral spacings. Within this viewpoint the everyday nature of social recognition becomes central to an understanding of the nature of urban moral spacings. Personal-stereo use demonstrates a structural negation of reciprocal forms of recognition as lying at the heart of everyday urban relations. Most urban and cultural literature fails to link these strands of experience and thereby fails to adequately incorporate an understanding of the qualitative nature of technologized experience in terms of the moral spacings of urban culture.

Within this context the aestheticization of the public through personal-stereo use can be understood both empirically and symbolically as a metaphor for wider social processes that resonate within personal-stereo use. Within the 'imaginary' of users is a negation of the present, of the world directly experienced and much of what it comprises. In this aestheticization the 'other' is denied as is any notion of 'difference'. The aesthetic becomes an attempt to hermetically seal off the outside world through a form of solipsistic experience maintenance. These motivations and strategies towards the everyday are, I have argued, part and parcel of the very culture from which they come.

The 'quality of the touch' existing between users and the social world is exemplified through modes of cognition, aesthetic or otherwise that appropriate the public in a manner that both prioritizes the user and fails to recognize notions of difference, thereby, in their moment of transcendence from the mundane features of their daily lifeworld, users embrace the cultural imperatives of public negation. They do so in order to inhabit a problematized subjective space mediated through the products of the 'social' that are simultaneously rejected or transformed. This paradox lies at the dialectical heart of the everyday experience of personal-stereo users.

Notes

1. Personal-stereo users each inhabit their own cultural 'bubble' facilitated by culturally produced messages from the 'dream pool' of culture. This demonstrates the need for an approach to the activity that does not reside solely in the realm of the individual nor totally in the structural realm. The filmic role in personal-stereo use is primarily orientated to forms of managing experience. The script of the aesthetics vary according to the purpose of the user. Whilst users do use a stock of messages, images and sounds to recreate their experiences it is necessary to look in more detail at the relationship between aesthetic recreation and structural determinants to any imaginary projection before reaching any premature conclusion over the evaluation of the potential determinant nature and origin of cultural 'dreampools'.

2. The use of the 'imaginary' in negating the apparent visual determinancy of the world is seen as having progressive tendencies by a diverse group of theorists from Nietzsche, Lukacs and Block to Benjamin and Adorno, in which the world transcending nature of the imaginary, the going beyond that which 'really' is, is referred to. In this act of 'going beyond' lies a utopian image or sensibility which can refer to the subject's view of 'life as it should be lived'. As such, the imaginary is potentially progressive from both a social and a political point of view. Benjamin, for example, points to modern forms of mass culture as representing both false consciousness and a source of phantasmagoria. It is in this very aspect of mass culture that the energy lies to overcome the prevailing conditions of society. Benjamin refers to the 'dreaming collective' as touching upon the re-enchantment of the industrial world. Alternatively, others have interpreted this strategy as merely retreating from the real into an

imaginary fabrication of both mood and feeling. By so doing the subject merely attempts to negate the uncertainty and open endedness of the world of experience. If one takes this position then the determinate negation of the visually present represents not an embodiment of freedom but a flight from contingency into a situation of safe habitation. Sartre brings out this quality of the imaginary in the following quote:

> to prefer the imaginary is not to prefer a richness, a beauty, an imaginary luxury to the existing mediocrity in spite of their real nature. It is also to adopt 'imaginary' feelings and actions for the sake of their imaginary nature. It is not only this or that image that is chosen, but the imaginary state with everything that it implies; it is not only an escape from the content of the real (poverty, frustrated love, failure of one's enterprises etc), but from the form of the real itself, its character of presences, the sort of response it demands of us, the adaptation of our actions to the object of inexhaustibility of perception, their independence, the way our feelings have of developing themselves. (Sartre 1992, p. 53)

This phenomenological viewpoint of Sartre represents a structural attempt to describe the phenomenology of the experiencing subject. However, Sartre's observations tends towards the ahistoric and non-specific in as much as 'the escape from the real' and the 'inexhaustibility of our perceptions' might vary in their specific historical and cultural phenomenological presences.

t h i r t e e n

Conclusion

This study has:

1. Provided a complex account of what is involved in the mediation of technology (personal stereos) and experience.
2. Investigated the relationship between forms of intention and contingency in the construction of everyday behaviour. In doing so it has identified and articulated a dialectic between structure and experience. For example, modes of saturation have been located in clearly identifiable situations in which personal-stereo users alleviate the passivity of the contingent through strategic forms of management. In doing so I have highlighted the construction of cognitive forms of instrumentalism within alienated forms and structures of everyday life.
3. Investigated the nature and role of the aural within urban everyday experience.
4. Constructed a critical phenomenology of personal-stereo use in order to explore the underlying meanings attached to use.
5. Re-evaluated the meanings attached to the management of auditory everyday experience by proposing a new critical framework informed by a reading of the early work of Critical Theorists.

   Throughout this book I have argued that cultural and urban theory has been unable to explain adequately the meanings attached to personal-stereo use. I am now in a position to produce a summary of the structural elements involved in personal-stereo use. I will do this by producing a typology of users' strategies together with an overview of personal stereo practices. The typology will both provide a useful way of understanding the complexity and breadth of analysis required in the study of personal-stereo use as well as indicating the inability of visually based epistemologies in providing just such an analysis. The typology should be read analytically, in the manner of a Weberian 'ideal type', as, empirically, one example can slide imperceptibly into another. Personal-stereo users are thus involved in the following strategies as they traverse urban space.

A Typology of Personal-Stereo Use

1. Users might be aiming to block out any external sound that they might otherwise hear in the street or elsewhere. The intrusion of any collection of aural sounds located within space is unwanted. They aim, through use, to replace the involuntary auditory sounds experienced in public space by their own personal soundscape placed directly between their ears. Personal stereos are very successful in displacing one set of auratic sensations with another. Urban dwellers know the city they live in and may dislike its loud, abrasive sound.

This type of scenario is very popular amongst urban theorists. Ever since the work of Simmel the common paradigm of urban behaviour has been framed in terms of urban sensory overload. I call this a variant of the urban retreating subjectivity theory. This boils down to the observation that we have to live in large, noisy cities and personal-stereo users don't like it! From this perspective, personal stereos function as an excellent tool as users attempt to reimpose control over the environment. Personal stereos thus permit users to control their environments.

2. Alternatively, but not in contradiction to the first point, users might experience discomfort in being surrounded by the faceless hordes of the city. They are jostled on the street, squashed against others on unkept and crowded tubes. Users experience difficulty in knowing where to place their eyes and are aware of their presence in the eyes of others and this makes them feel uncomfortable. In this explanation urban dwellers are reacting to the lack of personal space both bodily and visually. Personal stereos thus become a kind of mobile book or newspaper permitting users to attend to something else. In their absorption they can partially pretend that they are not really there. Personal stereos are more successful than these other objects as they permit the exclusion of the sound as well as the sight of these others.

From this point of view, personal stereos form an excellent boundary demarcator enabling the user to operationalize a range of strategies to negotiate crowded urban space. This perspective is as common as the first in accounts of urban experience and stems again from readings of the work of Simmel. The problematic presence of 'others' and the difficulty and need of establishing a zone of separateness also refers to notions of bourgeois civility highlighted by Simmel. This discomfort represents a bourgeois response to changing patterns of urban life that oblige strangers to spend large amounts of time in close proximity to one another in anonymous spaces. As urban cultures are becoming more privatized urban dwellers are perceived to be experiencing increased levels of discomfort as they traverse city spaces. As the technologies of the city in the form of public transport become oppressive, so personal stereos become a technological fix in alleviating this type of experience.

3. In contrast to the first two points, users often report using their personal stereos whenever they are alone in public. Users love to wear personal stereos whilst walking down deserted streets as well as in crowded high streets. Intrusion is a secondary issue in this type of use. Users describe being absorbed in the pleasure of listening unin-terruptedly to their own auditized flow of experience. These users prefer to hear their 'own' music whilst on the move. They may or may not take notice of their environment but more often than not they merely attend to their music. Personal-stereo use satisfies users' desires for their chosen sound accompaniment wherever they might be.

This type of usage differs from the first two, where users are primarily responding to their external environment. This type of usage rather indicates that users primarily are motivated by the desire to be accompanied by their own personalized music. Users often describe experiencing discomfort whilst on their own without 'their' music. As users are auditorily accompanied as they traverse social space, they feel 'better'. The fact that the music is 'personalized' often makes them feel special.

It appears that there is a specific relational quality of the auditory and its production of intimacy that needs investigating. Yet a trawl through urban- and cultural-studies texts will find no such analysis. Adorno is the only writer to have discussed the specifically auditory nature of urban relational experience, yet nobody appears to have noticed this as most cultural theorists never get further than discussing (negatively) his views on jazz. Yet Adorno provides a sophisticated account of states of 'we-ness' by which he means a reconfigured, technologized space in which users feels accompanied and not alone. Personal-stereo use provides the user with a sense of being 'connected'. It is also necessary to investigate the meanings attached to users' notions of 'personalized' as both personal stereos and what is listened to through them are, of course, industrial commodities.

4. Users sometimes describe their experience as particularly pleasurable, not necessarily as a response to loneliness, but as an aesthetic experience. Users often pick music to 'suit' the environment passed through. They may, for example, pick music that reminds them of what it is like to move through the city. For this type of usage to succeed it is important that the music is 'correct'. Failure often leads to frustration with the personal stereo being switch off. Users describe aesthetically recreating their environment through individually chosen music. Personal stereos used in this way permits the promotion of aesthetic or 'filmic' experience. This aestheticization creates the world as an imaginary space, a projection of the desire of the user formulated within the cultural remit of the stock of their imagination which is mediated through the attendant sounds listened to. This aestheticization of the urban is the dominant theme of existing work on personal stereos and is often referred to in terms of notions of *flânerie*. This concept, derived from the work of Benjamin, is often used in conjunction with postmodern accounts of urban dwelling in which the aesthetic is seen as a playful strategy of urban habitation in which de-centred subjectivities take pleasure in creative spatial redistribution. In this scenario, personal-stereo use is liberating. Images of *flânerie*, a visual form of experience, become translated onto auditory forms of experience.

Aestheticization is certainly an important user strategy. However, in contrast to 'flâneurs', personal-stereo users do not project themselves onto the world but rather construct the world narcissistically as a projection of their own 'mediated' sound world. This calls into question the meaning of the aestheticization of the urban together with the role of vision in the aestheticization process. It is necessary to ask what, if any, are the social implications of an auditory aesthetics as opposed to a primarily visual one in the construction of everyday urban behaviour.

5. Many personal-stereo users report that they are not particularly interested in their journey or their environment. What they particularly dislike about their daily routine are those parts of the day inhabited in 'no man's land'. They enjoy playing a tape that reminds them of something in their own narrative. As they listen they become absorbed with the flow of their memory sparked off by the sounds emanating from their personal stereo. They don't look, rather they recreate the feelings and sensations of whatever their memory conjures up before them. Personal-stereo use acts as a kind of auratic mnemonic. Users might be understood as discounting the urban through indifference (Sennett) and reformulating their experience through a sense of

'we-ness' (Adorno) articulated through the user's own imagined or reconstructed biography. Personal-stereo use thus enables users to attend to their own sense of narrative on the move.

6. This desire for re-establishing a place of mobile habitation need not be quite so literal as in the above example. Users might not particularly relish thinking about their own narrative. Rather they might feel an overwhelming sense of loneliness whilst on their own. They often report hating being alone, and the use of a personal stereo allays this. We recognize this type of behaviour very easily. Users are habitually accompanied with consumer technologies – they switch on the television as soon as they arrive home and they might go to sleep seduced by the auditized sounds of the radio. The street is the only place where they experience insecurity. The sounds and sights of the street are not enough to distract them from this awareness. The personal stereo gives users a sense of companionship. They 'know' their music and never feel 'alone' whilst listening to it. This is not identical to the desire for personalized music, as in example 3, rather the primary motive is to fend off feelings of isolation through the mediated company of personalized 'sounds'. Personal stereos provide company.

7. Users might not be responding to the perceived chaos of the urban environment as in examples 1 and 2, but to a sense of their own 'internal' chaos. Users often describe both the desire and the difficulty in ordering their thoughts appropriately. Unwanted feelings and thoughts flood in when they are on their own. Whilst at home users have television sets, music systems or the phone to organize or distract them. If not, there's always other people. The unadorned street or the tube cannot block out uncontrollable thoughts. Users often describe putting their personal stereos on as soon as they leave home with the purpose of 'clearing a space' for themselves. Use also helps them to change their mood in the desired direction. The 'space' in their head becomes tolerable enough to 'inhabit' once more. Personal stereos are mood managers that minimalize the contingency of users' thoughts, moods and emotions.

8. Users, most frequently female users, find that they are periodically pestered in public by others who intrude on their space. Using a personal stereo makes public space more easily inhabitable in these circumstances. They feel that other people do not trouble them so much as they are harder to approach. Users often describe feeling more confident in public wearing their personal stereos. Personal stereos are visual 'do not disturb' signs. They are also an efficient tool for control-ling the manner and nature of contact with others. Users will often

describe talking and listening simultaneously. They sometimes even pretend to listen. Personal stereos are personal boundary demarcators and interpersonal mediators.

9. City life is often experienced as repetitive and users are often consumed with their oppressive routine. They describe taking the same journey to work every weekday, forty-eight weeks of the year. They might also be fed up and bored with their job, their routine and their journey. They know each step of the daily journey with its predictable monotony, every station and how long it will take them to cover their daily journey. They feel oppressed by it. They have long ceased to take any notice of their surroundings. The use of a personal stereo is the only thing that makes the time pass bearably for these users. At least whilst they listen to it they do not have to think about their daily routine or the office that awaits them. Personal stereos permit users to reclaim or repossess time.

10. Personal-stereo users often feel a greater sense of purpose as they stride out into the street. They describe feeling energized. The music, with its steady rhythm, helps them in this. Their body and the sound appear as one. The physical nature of the world is recessed. Personal stereos are activators.

11. User are not always alone. Sometimes they share their personal stereo with a friend, both listening by sharing one headphone. They listen, both attentive and absorbed by the sounds of the personal stereo. Personal stereos constitute a form of 'group' exclusivity.

The typology explains the necessity for my auditory epistemology of urban experience produced in the previous chapters. Visually based theories of urban experience only adequately describe the first two examples of the typology. In example 4 a visual epistemology leads to a mistaken understanding of the nature of an auditory aesthetic. The construction of a critical phenomenology of personal-stereo use has also enabled me to produce a set of fresh insights into the meanings underlying everyday auditory experience, thus permitting a critical evaluation of the nature of the moral spacings of that behaviour. I will now summarize these strategies, together with an evaluation of their significance, in the following pages.

Phenomenological Overview of Personal-Stereo Practices

I have demonstrated the way in which personal-stereo users construct large areas of their everyday life through the use of their machines.

Personal-stereo use becomes 'second nature' to many users in their negotiation of everyday urban life. Auditory 'looking' was systematically analysed whereby users were demonstrated as operationalizing a range of visual strategies that were both aesthetic and non-aesthetic. Many of these strategies of 'looking' were found to involve an avoidance of reciprocal looking or interaction. 'Looking' took place within a privatized and auditized soundtrack that constituted states of 'being with' that were operationalized within a range of aesthetic modes of orientation that heightened the natures of both the urban and the user's own interior experience. The form that this aestheticization took varied in its visual meaning and significance. The aesthetic often referred to an 'interior' flow of experience in which the 'visual' often had minimal significance. Alternatively, users transformed or appropriated urban space by integrating it into their aesthetic fantasies.

Non-aesthetic strategies of looking were investigated as part and parcel of everyday personal-stereo use in which users were portrayed as engaging in multiple strategies of controlling the 'gaze' through the establishment of zones of separation constituted through the subjective auditory nature of the personal stereo. Geographical notions of personal space were thus discounted by being reinscribed as a 'private' conceptual space in which the personal stereo acted as a facilitator for solipsistic strategies of empowerment in which the user's 'gaze' was both empowered and non-reflective.

This reconceptualization of the space of habitation through personal-stereo use was also embodied in users' strategies of placing themselves 'elsewhere' in urban environments, thereby making the reception of the 'other's' gaze more difficult to receive. In doing so, the study demonstrated that the negation of the public was attended to by a prioritization of a technologically mediated private realm for personal-stereo users. This reprioritization of subjective experience was also demonstrated as being operative in a range of interpersonal behaviours whereby users described using their personal stereos both as a form of communication demarcator and as a communication enhancer. Personal-stereo users' sense of self-prioritization was described as being enhanced through the power to disengage at will from a variety of forms of interaction. Forms of face-to-face interaction were described as continually being in competition with simulated forms of experience, with users often finding the simulated as being more attractive than the face-to-face. When used collectively, the personal stereo formed a collective communication demarcator that also facilitated the continuation of discourse through multiple strategies of talk interspersed with listening and comment.

A transformed site of experience through personal-stereo use was analysed through notions of habitation that focused upon the site of experience as a form of 'sanctuary' representing a progressive privatization of the experiencing subject. Within this 'sanctuary', personal-stereo users both prioritized and centred their experience. Personal narratives were constructed through the construction of forms of auditory mnemonics. These strategies permitted the user to transcend geometrical space and reconstitute an imaginary space of personal narrative. The nature of this technologized space was experienced as all engulfing, enabling the space of habitation to be infused with its own sense of heightened experiential aura. The manufactured aura of personal-stereo use reinscribed space and time with significance and permanence, 'monumentalizing' it. This reinscribing transformed the perceived void or oppressiveness of empirical space and time described by personal-stereo users, by facilitating forms of management that minimized their apprehension of contingency. Personal-stereo users were described as existing through forms of accompanied solitude constructed through a manufactured industrialized auditory. Personal-stereo use was seen as colonizing the space of users thereby working to transform their mood, orientation and reach so as to provide them with a sense of empowerment, coherence and narrative, precisely by negating the contingent nature of experience, both geographically and volitionally. Users described the pushing away of a range of unwanted thoughts and feelings through use, thereby managing their own cognition through technology. Personal-stereo users were demonstrated to have a greater sense of control over areas of urban experience previously considered immune from control. The exclusion of all forms of intrusion constituted a successful strategy for urban and personal management.

In this pursuit of minimizing contingency, personal-stereo use became both a clarifier and a simplifier of experience. Mood was maintained and controlled over time through the choice of sound to be attended to and the manner of use. Headspace thus became both saturated and hermetically sealed whereby levels of stress were managed and the flow of thoughts and emotions directed. The above analysis clearly shows the benefit of using a critically inspired phenomenological analysis to understand personal-stereo use. In doing so I have been able to reformulate the meanings attached to such behaviour and to develop new categories of everyday behaviour, such as investigating the nature of auditory looking. In doing so I have been able to address the specific relational qualities attached to technologized auditory everyday experience so often overlooked in urban and cultural studies.

Technology, Contingency and Everyday Life: A Few Concluding Remarks

The analysis of personal-stereo use has demonstrated a range of experiential strategies and orientations that cast light on the social construction of everyday experience. However, the dividing line between the 'public' and the maintenance of a 'private' realm has proven to be dialectically linked as mediated private realms have been demonstrated as increasingly existing in public spaces. Personal-stereo users both present themselves via technology and construct the social via technology. The analysis of personal-stereo use has permitted an evaluation of those strategies that is not merely descriptive. For example, an evaluation of the strategies employed in managing and controlling the gaze, or a description of the anxiety experienced when personal-stereo users find themselves without the use of their personal stereos, demonstrates the fragility of users' everyday experience. Personal-stereo users do not display a confidence concerning themselves or the socially unadorned. Rather, experience becomes both manageable and significant precisely through the technologizing of that experiential flow. Personal-stereo use represents an example of the technologizing of experience within which a range of strategies are operationalized which I have characterized in terms of social asymmetry. Forms of experiential asymmetry have not been described in neutral terms in this study but have rather pointed to an evaluation of the fragility of everyday urban experience. One dominant form of asymmetry located in personal-stereo use has been the aestheticization of the 'social'. I have argued that this aestheticization itself reflects an orientation to the everyday that is deeply embedded in Western modes of cognition that deny otherness through the appropriation of experience into forms of solipsistic transcendence. This, in effect, means a turning away from the geographical and social present. Instead users construct safe technologized habitats where users experience time and place through dwelling within an interiority that is itself made habitable only through cultural mediation.

The use of personal stereos can be usefully described as a 'device paradigm' whereby subjects withdraw from 'the manifold engagement with things' that surround them (Taylor 1995). The process is a dialectical one in which users withdraw in order to 'be with' a mediated elsewhere desired by and fulfilled through personal-stereo use. The discounting of the public nature of the urban into a reconfigured personalized private in the public does not merely relate to issues of space–time compression (Harvey 1996) but rather to a re-embedding of space and time whereby everyday experience is reconfigured with a personalized meaning. Such meanings are, as has been demonstrated, themselves appropriated from moments embodied in the products of the culture industry. The lived experiential manner of these strategies can be understood through Foucault's notion of heterotopia in which the subject creates a space for themselves beyond or outside surveillance. This notion of heterotopia can itself be understood dialectically in as much as the subject opens themselves up via mediation in order to enact successful strategies of social closure (Foucault 1986). This mediated space 'beyond' becomes part of a technologized device paradigm in which the subject lives. Bauman does not quite capture the meaning of this strategy of urban spatial management:

> One could pursue radical solutions of city life ambivalence following one of two 'rational' (though equally self defeating) strategies. One is to drastically reduce, or eliminate altogether, the element of surprise, and thus unpredictability, in the conduct of strangers. The other is to devise ways and means to render that element of contingency irrelevant, to blend the movement of strangers into the background one need neither notice or care about. (Bauman 1991, p. 130)

Personal-stereo use is more appropriately understood as embodying a denial of contingency embedded in the experience of time. The motivation for this has less to do with the concern with strangers as described by Bauman as by a joint imperative of denial of the public (Sennett 1990) and as a form of atomistic subjective expressiveness and instrumentalism (Taylor 1995). The user thus gains a sense of a heightened awareness of their own fragile contingency through strategies that manage or deny this state through the embracing of states of 'we-ness'.

The analysis of personal-stereo use has indicated that it is necessary to link the nature of auratic forms of experience embodied in personal-stereo use to a set of relational concerns within the analysis of urban experience by focusing upon a qualitative assessment of a technologized site and horizon of experience. These processes are best understood dialectically, not dichotomously. Therefore subjects are understood as being neither free nor colonized but as existing in a dialectical and often ambivalent relation to both. Throughout the analysis of personal-stereo use I have articulated the ambivalent nature of strategies employed by users in their management of everyday life.

A defining feature of personal-stereo use is its technological nature. The study demonstrates that urban experience has in fact become an increasingly technological experience. As personal-stereo users move through urban space their experience is intrinsically technological experience. Technology is of course social and in important respects the social is already technological. Throughout this work I have understood technological artifacts in terms of, and through, the experiencing subject. Personal-stereo use demonstrates that both technology and experience is always mediated. Everyday behaviour is an assemblage which need not be understood in terms of forms of technological dualism. In articulating the strategies that users undertake in relation to the management of their everyday experience, I have highlighted their mediated and instrumental nature whereby forms of social asymmetry embedded in habitual everyday behaviour form a constituent part of users' everyday lives. In analysing social practices thus, I have not viewed personal stereos simply as an artifact that has a range of properties and effects attached to it (essentialism), neither have I understood it merely as a text (anti-essentialism). Essentialism tends to void agency or at best relates it to structure, whereas anti-essentialism tends to void structure implying subjective authority over objects. Rather than locating meaning either in use or in structure, I have articulated a dialectical relationship between them. Technologies are themselves embedded in social structures and social systems and the manner and significance of this embeddedness can be articulated through an analysis of everyday forms of usage. Embodied in these practices is a set of tacit assumptions about experience and its relationship to the world. The manner in which these values are embedded and how they assert themselves in forms of social behaviour has been a central concern of this work. It is hoped that this work will at least encourage other writers in the field to recognize the role of auditory experience in everyday life, and that it will encourage them not to fall back on traditional concepts of explanation that are themselves in need of either interrogation or transcendence.

Bibliography

Adorno, T. (1941a) 'The Radio Symphony'. *Radio Research* 1941. Edited by Paul Lazarsfeld and Frank Stanton. New York: Duell, Slone and Pierce.

Adorno, T. (1941b) 'On Popular Music'. *Studies in Philosophy and the Social* Sciences 9: 17–48.

Adorno, T. (1941c) 'The Radio Symphony: An Experiment in Theory'. *Radio Research* 1941. Edited by Paul Lazarsfeld and Frank Stanton. New York: Duell, Slone and Pierce.

Adorno, T. (1945) 'A Social Critique of Radio Music', *Kenyon Review* 7: 208–17.

Adorno, T. (1964) *The Authoritarian Personality*. New York. John Wiley.

Adorno, T. (1967) 'Psychology and Sociology'. *New Left Review*. 47: 79–97.

Adorno, T. (1973) *The Philosophy of Modern Music*. London. Sheed and Ward.

Adorno, T. (1974). *Minima Moralia: Reflections on a Damaged Life*. London. New Left Books. Adorno, T. (1976a) *Introduction to the Sociology of Music*. New York. Continuum Press.

Adorno, T. (1976b) *The Positivist Dispute in German Sociology*. London. Heinemann.

Adorno, T. (1977) 'The Actuality of Philosophy'. *Telos* 31: 120–33.

Adorno, T. (1990a) 'The Curves of the Needle'. *October*. 55: 49–55.

Adorno, T. (1990b) 'The Form of the Phonograph Record.' *October*. 55: 56–61.

Adorno, T. (1991) *The Culture Industry: Selected Essays on Mass Culture*. London. Routledge.

Adorno, T. (1992) 'Fetish Character in Music and Regressive Listening'.

Adorno, T. (1994) *The Stars down to Earth*. London. Routledge.

Adorno, T. (1998) *Critical Models: Interventions and Catchwords*. New York. Columbia University Press.

Adorno, T. and Eisler, H. (1994) *Composing for the Films*. London. Athlone.

Agger, B. (1992) *The Discourse of Domination*. Evanston. Northwestern University Press.

Ang, I. (1985) *Watching Dallas*. London. Methuen.

Appadurai, A. (1986) *The Social Life of Things: Commodities in Cultural Perspective*. Cambridge. Cambridge University Press.

Arato, A. and Gebhardt, E. (eds) (1992) *The Essential Frankfurt School Reader*. New York. Continuum Press.

Attali, J. (1985) *Noise: The Political Economy of Music*. Minneapolis. University of Minnesota Press.

Bachelard, G. (1994) *The Poetics of Space: The Classical Look at how we Experience Intimate Places*. Boston. Beacon Press.

Baudrillard, J. (1993) *Symbolic Exchange and Death*. London. Sage.

Bauman, Z. (1988) *The Consequences of Modernity*. Cambridge. Polity Press.

Bauman, Z (1991) *Modernity and Ambivalence*. Cambridge. Polity Press.

Bauman, Z. (1993) *Postmodern Ethics*. Oxford. Blackwell.

Bauman, Z. (1994) 'Desert Spectacular' in Tester. *The Flâneur*. London. Routledge.

Beilharz, P. Robinson, G. and Rundell, J. (eds) (1992) *Between Totalitarianism and Postmodernity*. Cambridge, Mass. MIT Press.

Benhabib, S. (1986) *Critique, Norm, and Utopia*. Columbia University Press.

Benhabib, S. Bonb, W. and McCole, J. (eds) (1993) *On Max Horkheimer. New Perspectives*. Cambridge, Mass. MIT Press.

Benjamin, W. (1973a) *Charles Baudelaire: A Lyric Poet in the Era of High Capitalism*. London. New Left Books.

Benjamin, W. (1973b) *Illuminations*. London. Penguin.

Benjamin, W. (1986) *Reflections: Essays, Aphorisms, Autobiographical Writings*. ed. P. Demetz. New York. Schocken Books.

Benjamin, W. (1991) *Gesammelte Schriften, vols 1–7*. Suhrkamp Verlag. Frankfurt.

Benjamin. W. (1999) *Selected Writings. Volume 2: 1927–1934*. Cambridge, Mass: Harvard University Press.

Bernstein, R. (1991) *The New Constellation*. Cambridge. Polity Press.

Bijker, E. W. (1997) *Of Bicycles, Bakelites, and Bulbs: Toward a Theory of Sociotechnical Change*. Cambridge, Mass. MIT Press.

Bloch, E. (1986) *The Principle of Hope. Vols. 1, 2, and 3*. Oxford. Blackwell Press.

Bloch, E. (1988) *The Utopian Function of Art in Literature*. Cambridge,

Mass. MIT Press.

Bloch, E. (1991) *Heritage of our Times*. Cambridge. Polity Press.

Bokina, J. and Lukes, J. (eds) (1994) *Marcuse: From the New Left to the Next Left*, Lawrence, Kans. University Press of Kansas

Born. G. (1995) *Rationalizing Culture. IRCAM, Boulez, and the Institutionalization of the Musical Avant-Garde*. Berkeley. University of California Press.

Brodersen, M. (1996) *Walter Benjamin*. London. Verso.

Buck-Morss, S. (1991) *The Dialectics of Seeing: Walter Benjamin and the Arcades Project*. Cambridge, Mass. MIT Press

Burgin, V. (1996) *In/Different spaces: Place and Memory in Visual Culture*. Berkeley. University of California Press.

Calhoun, C. (1992) *Habermas and the Public Sphere*. Cambridge, Mass. MIT Press.

Calhoun, C. (1995) *Critical Social Theory*. Oxford. Blackwell.

Callon, M. and Latour, B. (1981) 'Unscrewing the Big Leviathan, or How do Actors Macrostructure Reality?' in K.D. Knorr-Cetina and A. Cicourel, eds. *Advances in Social Theory and Methodology toward an Integration of Micro- and Macro-Sociologies*. London. Routledge & Kegan Paul.

Cashmore, E. (1994) *And then there was Television*. London. Routledge

Caygill, H. (1998) *Walter Benjamin: The Colour of Experience*. London. Routledge.

Chambers, I. (1994) *Migrancy, Culture, Identity*. London. Routledge.

Clarke, D. (ed.) (1997) *The Cinematic City*. London. Routledge.

Cohen, S. and Taylor, L. (1976) *Escape Attempts*. London. Routledge.

Connor, S. (1997) 'The Modern Auditory I'. in R. Porter. *Rewriting the Self: Histories from the Renaissance to the Present*. London. Routledge.

Crary, J. (1992) *Techniques of the Observer*. Cambridge, Mass. MIT Press.

Debord, G. (1977) *Society of the Spectacle*. Detroit. Black and Red.

De Certeau, M. (1988) *The Practice of Everyday Life*. Berkeley. California University Press.

Deleuze, G. and Felix Guattari (1987) *A Thousand Plateaus*. Minneapolis. University of Minnesota Press

DeLillo, D. (1988) *Libra*. London. Penguin.

Denzin, N. K. (1995) *The Cinematic Society*. London. Sage.

du Gay, P. and Hall, S. (eds) (1997) *Doing Cultural Studies: The Story of the Sony Walkman*. London. Sage Duncan, N. (ed.) (1996) *Body Space: Destabalising Geographies of Gender and Sexuality*. London. Routledge.

Eco, U. (1994) *How to Travel with a Salmon*. London. Minerva.

Fiske, J. (1989) *Reading the Popular*. London. Unwin Hayman

Flinn, C. (1992) *Strains of Utopia: Gender, Nostalgia, and Hollywood Music*. Princeton. Princeton University Press.

Foucault, M. (1986) 'Heterotopias'. Diacritics. Spring: 22–27.

Freidberg, A. (1993) *Window Shopping*. Berkeley. California University Press. Frisby, D. (1985) *Fragments of Modernity: Theories of Modernity in the Work of Simmel, Kracauer and Benjamin*. Cambridge. Polity Press.

Frisby, D. (1992) *Simmel and Since: Essays on Georg Simmel's Social Theory*. London. Routledge.

Frisby, D. and Featherstone. M. (eds) (1997) *Simmel on Culture*. London. Sage.

Fromm, E. (1984) *The Working Class in Weimar Germany*. London. Berg.

Gibson, W. (1993) *Time Out*. 6 October: 49.

Giddens, A. (1991) *Modernity and Self Identity*. Cambridge. Polity Press. Gilloch, G. (1996) *Myth and Metropolis: Walter Benjamin and the City*. Cambridge. Polity Press.

Goffman, E. (1969) *The Presentation of Self in Everyday Life*. London. Penguin.

Goffman, E. (1971) *Relations in Public: Microstudies of Public Order*. London. Penguin.

Goldthorpe, J. and Lockwood, D. (1968–9) *The Affluent Worker. Vols 1, 2 and 3*. Cambridge: Cambridge University Press

Grint, K., and Woolgar, S. (eds) (1997) *The Machine at Work*. Cambridge. Polity Press.

Grivel, C. (1992) 'The Phonograph's Horned Mouth'. in Kahn and Whitehead. *Wireless Imagination*. Cambridge. MIT Press.

Habermas. J. (1987) *The Philosophical Discourse of Modernity*. Cambridge. Polity. Habermas, J. (1989) *The Structural Transformation of the Public Sphere: An Inquiry into a Category of Bourgeois Society*. Cambridge. Polity.

Habermas, J. (1995) *Justification and Application*. Cambridge. Polity.

Hall, S. and du Gay, P. (eds) (1996) *Questions of Cultural Identity*. London. Sage.

Hansen, M. (1987) 'Benjamin, Cinema and Experience: "The Blue Flower in the Land of Technology"'. *New German Critique* 40: 51–89.

Hansen, M. (1991) *Babylon and Babel: Spectatorship in American Silent Film*. Cambridge, Mass. Harvard University Press.

Harvey, D. (1990) *The Condition of Postmodernity*. London. Blackwell.

Harvey, D. (1996.) *Justice, Nature and the Geography of Difference*. Oxford. Blackwell

Hays, K.M. (1992) *Modernism and the Posthumanist Subject: The Architecture of Hannes Meyer and Ludwig Hilberseimer*. Cambridge, Mass. MIT Press.

Hebdige, D. (1988) *Hiding in the Light*. London. Comedia.

Heidegger, M. (1978) *Basic Writings*. London. Routledge.

Hohendahl, P.U. (1995) *Prismatic Thought: Theodor W. Adorno*. Lincoln, Nebr. University of Nebraska Press.

Honneth, A. (1992) 'Pluralization and Recognition: On the Self-Misuderstanding of Postmodern Social Theorists', in P. Beilharz, G. Robinson and J. Rundell. *Between Totalitarianism and Postmodernity*. Cambridge, Mass. MIT Press.

Honneth, A. (1993) *The Critique of Power*. Cambridge, Mass. MIT Press.

Honneth, A. (1995a) *The Fragmented World of the Social: Essays in Social and Political Philosophy*. New York. Sunny Press.

Honneth, A. (1995b) *The Struggle for Recognition: The Moral Grammar of Social Conflicts*. Cambridge. Polity Press.

Horkheimer, M. (1972) *Critical Theory*. New York. Herder & Herder.

Horkheimer, M. (1974) *Critique of Instrumental Reason*. New York. Seabury Press. Horkheimer, M. and Adorno, T. (1973) *The Dialectic of Enlightenment*. London. Penguin.

Hosokawa, S. (1984) 'The Walkman Effect'. *Popular Music* 4: 165–80.

Hoy, D.C. and McCarthy. T (1994) *Critical Theory*. Oxford. Blackwell Press.

Huhn, T. and Zuidervaart, L. (eds) (1997) *The Semblance of Subjectivity: Essays in Adorno's Aesthetic Theory*. Cambridge, Mass. MIT Press.

Ihde, D. (1993) *Postphenomenology: Essays in a Postmodern Context*. Evanston. Northwestern University Press.

Jameson, F. (1991) *Postmodernism, or The Cultural Logic of Late Capitalism*. London. Verso.

Jay, M. (1973) *The Dialectical Imagination*. London. Heinemann Press.

Jay, M. (1984) *Marxism and Totality*. Cambridge. Polity Press.

Jay, M. (1993) *Downcast Eyes: The Denigration of Vision in Twentieth-Century French Thought*. Berkeley. University of California Press.

Jenks, C. (ed.) (1995) *Visual Culture*. London. Routledge.

Kahn, D. and Whitehead, G. (eds) (1992) *Wireless Imagination: Sound, Radio and the Avant-Garde*. Cambridge, Mass. MIT Press.

Kellner, D. (1995) *Media and Culture*. London. Routledge.

Kittler. F. (1999) *Gramophone, Film, Typewriter*. Stanford. Stanford University Press.

Kolb, D. (1986) *The Critique of Pure Modernity: Hegel, Heidegger and After*. Chicago. University of Chicago Press.

Kracauer, S. (1995) *The Mass Ornament: Weimar Essays*. Cambridge, Mass. Harvard University Press.

Lash, S. and Urry, J. (1995) *Economies of Signs and Space*. London. Sage.

Lefebvre, H. (1991a) *A Critique of Everyday Life*. London. Verso.

Lefebvre, H. (1991b) *The Production of Space*. Oxford. Blackwell.

Lefebvre, H. (1996) *Writings on Cities*. Oxford. Blackwell.

Levin, D. M. (1985) *The Body's Recollection of Being*. London. Routledge & Kegan Paul.

Levin, D. M. (1988) *The Opening of Vision: Nihilism and the Postmodern Situation*. London. Routledge.

Levin, T. Y. (1990) 'Music in the Age of its Technological Reproducability'. October 55: 23–47.

Lull, J. (1990) *Inside Family Viewing*. London. Routledge.

Malbon, B. (1998) 'Consumption, Identity and the Spatial Practices of Everynight Life' in T. Skelton and G. Valentine. *Cool Places*. London. Routledge.

Marcuse, H. (1972a) *Negations*. London. Penguin

Marcuse, H. (1972b) *One Dimensional Man*. London. Acabus.

Marcuse, H. (1973) *Five Lectures*. London. Penguin.

Marx, K. (1964) *Economic and Philosophical Manuscript*. New York. International Press

Massey, D. (1994) *Space, Place and Gender*. Cambridge. Polity Press.

McCarthy, T. (1993) *Ideals and Illusions: On Reconstruction and Deconstruction in Contemporary Critical Theory*. Cambridge, Mass. MIT Press.

McGuigan, J. (ed.) (1997) *Cultural Methodologies*. London. Sage.

Mehlman, J. (1993) *Walter Benjamin for Children: An Essay on his Radio Years*. Chicago. University of Chicago Press.

Merleau-Ponty, M. (1964) *The Primacy of Perception*. Evanston, Ill. Northwestern University Press.Miller, P. (1987) *Domination and Power*. London. Routledge.

Moebius, H. and Michel-Annen, B. (1994) 'Colouring the Grey Everyday: The Psychology of the Walkman'. *Free Associations* 4.4.32: 570–7.

Moores, S. (1993) *Interpreting Audiences: The Ethnography of Media Consumption*. London. Sage.

Morley, D. (1992) *Television, Audiences and Cultural Studies*. London. Routledge.

Mustenberg, H. (1970) *The Film: A Psychological Study*. New York. Dover Publications.

Nagel, T. (1986) *The View from Nowhere*. Oxford. Oxford University Press.

Natanson, M. (ed.) (1969) *Essays in Phenomenology*. The Hague. Nijhoff.

Natanson, M. (1976)'Introduction' to *Schutz: Collected Papers. Vol 1: The Problem of Social Reality*. The Hague. Nijhoff.

Negt, O. and Kluge, A. (1993) *Public Sphere and Experience*. Minneapolis. University of Minnesota Press.

Nicholsen, S.W. (1997) *Exact Imagination: Late Work on Adorno's Aesthetics*. Cambridge, Mass. MIT Press.Ohsone, K. (1988) *The Case of the Walkman*. Tokyo. Sony Corporation.Osborne, P. (1995) *The Politics of Time: Modernity and the Avante Garde*. London. Verso.

Paddison, M. (1993) *Adorno's Aesthetic of Music*. Cambridge. Cambridge University Press.

Pile, S. (1996) *The Body and the City: Psychoanalysis, Space and Subjectivity*. London. Routledge.

Poster, M. (1995) *The Second Media Age*. London. Polity Press.

Prendergast, C. (1992) *Paris and the Nineteenth Century*. Oxford. Blackwell.Provenzo, E. (1991) *Video Kids: Making Sense of Nintendo*. Cambridge, Mass. Harvard University

Press. R. J. (1999) *I See a Voice: Language, Deafness and the Senses, A Philosophical Enquiry*. HarperCollins. London.

Rojek, C. (1995) *Decentring Leisure*. London. Sage.

Rojek, C. and Urry, J. (eds) (1994) *Touring Cultures: Transformations of Travel and Theory*. London. Routledge

Sachs, W. (1992) *For Love of the Automobile: Looking Back into the History of our Desires*. Berkeley. University of California Press.

Sartre, J.-P. (1966) *Being and Nothingness: A Phenomenological Essay on Ontology*. New York. Washington Square Press.

Sartre, J.-P. (1992) Truth and Existence. Chicago. University of Chicago Press.

Schutz, A. and Luckmann, T. (1983) *The Structures of the Life World*. Vol. 2. Evanston, Ill. Northwestern University Press.

Selnow, R. (1984) 'Playing Video Games: The Electronic Friend'. *Journal of Communication* 34: 58–72.

Sennett, R. (1977) *The Fall of Public Man*. London. Faber and Faber.

Sennett, R. (1990) *The Conscience of the Eye*. London. Faber and Faber.

Sennett, R. (1994) *Flesh and Stone*. New York. Norton.

Silverstone, R. (1994) Television and Everyday Life. London. Routledge.

Silverstone, R. and Hirsch, E. (eds) (1992) *Consuming Technologies: Media and Information in Domestic Spaces*. London. Routledge.

Simmel, G. (1997a) 'The Metropolis and Mental Life'. in Frisby and Featherstone (eds). *Simmel on Culture*.

Simmel, G. (1997b) 'Sociology of the Senses'. in Frisby and Featherstone (eds). *Simmel on Culture*.

Simpson, L. C. (1995) *Technology, Time and the Conversations of Modernity*. London. Routledge.

Skelton, T. and Valentine, G. (eds) (1998) *Cool places: Geographies of Youth Cultures*. London. Routledge.

Smith, G. (ed.) (1991) *On Walter Benjamin*. Cambridge, Mass. MIT Press.

Soja, E. (1996) *Thirdspace: Journeys to Los Angeles and Other Real and Imagined Places*. Oxford. Blackwell.

Stone, A. C. (1995) *The War of Desire and Technology at the Close of the Mechanical Age*. Cambridge, Mass. MIT Press

Tacussel, P. (1986) 'The City, the Player: Walter Benjamin and the Origins of Figurative Sociology. *Diogenes*, 134: 45–59.

Taylor, C. (1989) *Sources of the Self: The Making of Modern Identity*. Cambridge. Cambridge University Press.

Taylor, C. (1995) *Philosophical Arguments*. Cambridge, Mass. Harvard University Press. Tester, K. (ed.) (1994) *The Flâneur*. London. Routledge.

Thompson, J. (1990) *Ideology and Modern Culture*. Stanford. Stanford University Press.

Thornton, S. (1995) *Club Cultures: Music, Media and Subcultural Capital*. London. Polity Press.

Turkle, S. (1995) *Life on the Screen: Identity in the Age of the Internet*. New York. Simon & Schuster.

Virilio, P. (1989) *War and Cinema*, London. Verso.

Welsch, W. (1997) *Undoing Aesthetics*. London. Routledge.

Westwood, S. and Williams, J. (eds) (1997) *Imagining Cities: Scripts, Signs and Memory*. London. Routledge.

Wiggerhaus, R. (1994) *The Frankfurt School*. Cambridge. Polity Press.

Williams, R. (1977) *Resources of Hope*, Culture, Democracy, Socialism. London Verso.

Williamson, J. (1990) 'Consuming Passions'. in P. Jukes. *A Shout in the Street*. London. Faber & Faber.

Witkin, R. (1998) *Adorno on Music*. London. Routledge.

Wolin, R. (1994) *Walter Benjamin: An Aesthetic of Redemption*. Berkeley. California University Press.

Zimmerman, M. (1990) *Heidegger's Confrontation with Modernity*. Ithaca. Indiana University Press.

Zizek, S. (1997) *The Plague of Fantasies*. London. Verso.

Zuidervaart, L. (1991) *Adorno's Aesthetic Theory: The Redemption of Illusion*. Cambridge, Mass. MIT Press.

Index